CHOOSING LOVE

Life is a series of choices, most of them so small we scarcely realize that we're making them. Or why. Sometimes we call them "reactions" and disclaim responsibility for them, not recognizing that reactions are choices, too. We seldom give thought to where these small, secret choices are taking us and whether or not we want to go there.

Most of the man-meets-woman, man-loses-woman plots of films and television come from the premise that love is a feeling that just happens. Or else it doesn't happen. Or it happens and then stops happening, so that nothing can be done to recapture the feeling once it goes.

The truth is that love is an active power which you were meant to control with your own will. You are not "just a prisoner of love," as the song claims. You can choose to love your marriage partner moment by moment, no matter what the circumstances are, or how you are feeling.

TWENTY STEPS TO A STRONGER, HEALTHIER MARRIAGE

SECRET CHOICES

ED WHEAT, M.D.
and Gloria Okes Perkins

HarperPaperbacks
Zondervan Publishing House
Divisions of HarperCollinsPublishers

HarperPaperbacks   *A Division of* HarperCollins*Publishers*
                   10 East 53rd Street, New York, N.Y. 10022

A trade paperback edition of this book was published in
1989 by Zondervan Publishing House, a division of
HarperCollins*Publishers*.

First HarperPaperbacks printing: July 1994

Printed in the United States of America

HarperPaperbacks and colophon are trademarks of
HarperCollins*Publishers*

❖ 10 9 8 7 6 5 4 3 2 1

With thanksgiving for my wonderful dad and mother,
Guy and Irene Okes, who have shown me the reality of
their faith in Jesus Christ, and the generosity of their love,
without end

Gloria Okes Perkins

CONTENTS

Part Four: What Resources Are You Depending On?

PREFACE

Secret Choices continues the adventure we began last year with the writing of *The First Years of Forever,* a handbook for newlyweds with high expectations of happiness and the enthusiasm to commit themselves to the process of building a wonderful, lasting marriage.

We made it our prayerful goal to offer, in one volume, the hard-to-obtain, new-marriage counsel that every couple needs at the beginning of their life together. We included the essentials for building a *forever* relationship: understanding and guarding the feelings of love; living by the facts of love; learning the principles of faithfulness and forgiveness; building the lifeline system of good communication; discovering the secrets of sexual fulfillment; and recognizing warning signals. Most importantly, we provided complete handbooks for husbands and wives with specific biblical counsel on *how* to love each other in the ways most needed and desired.

Even so, much remained to be said, which we could not fit into one volume. We knew, also, that couples, still caught up in the wonder of their love, are not ready to take in every principle of marriage at the beginning. With a little experience comes a greater awareness of potential problems and the desire to learn how to deal with the unexpected challenges of marriage.

So we invited our readers to participate in a second book to be used as a companion to *The First Years of*

Forever. We asked them to share their experiences with us, their questions and discoveries. *Secret Choices: Personal Decisions That Affect Your Marriage* is the result. We believe you will find, as we have, that these Bible-based concepts, when applied, will change the quality of your marriage and your life.

And the adventure goes on. Let us hear from you at *Secret Choices,* P.O. Box 410, Springdale, Arkansas 72764.

> Your friends in Christ,
> Ed Wheat, M.D. and Gloria Okes Perkins

ACKNOWLEDGMENTS

Our thanks to

George Fooshee, Dow Pursley, and Victoria James, whose wonderful contributions enriched our book;

our friend and pastor, John Glasser, for his timely and well-seasoned comments;

and all our friends and loved ones who prayed.

SECRET CHOICES

The choices that determine the success of your marriage are secret ones because they happen on the inside first. Later, the results can be seen by all.

INTRODUCTION

All of us know, as a matter of practical experience that there is something within us, behind our emotions, and behind our wishes, an independent self, that, after all, decides everything.

Hannah Whitall Smith

We usually approach major decisions as though they were packages marked: *Handle with care.* But what about the small personal choices we exercise from moment to moment, scarcely realizing we've just made a choice? Do we ever ask ourselves, *What are we really choosing? Where might this take us? Do we want to go in that direction?* We should!

Within the sensitive setting of marriage these small choices have more power to bless or hurt a relationship than we could imagine. For all their seeming unimportance, they carry long-term consequences and ultimately can make the difference between success in building a love-filled marriage or failure.

In this fourth book of marriage counsel, we have a compelling truth to share with you: *Your secret choices have power. You can learn to use them to determine the success of your marriage.* Forget the theory that "if it's meant to work out, it will." Yes, God wants your marriage to succeed, but He has entrusted your relationship into your own care. Please don't hand it over to "fate," "luck," or "wishful thinking." The responsibility—and the benefits—are all yours.

In the next fourteen chapters you will discover how to become aware of your choices and their consequences; how to take charge of them; and how to make the best choices to create the right emotional climate in your marriage and establish an enjoyable partnership that really works. You will also find biblical counsel and spiritual resources to help you explore your potential for growth and positive change.

As you read, watch for the "stepping stones." These enclosed blocks of copy will give you twenty steps to follow in your quest for a marriage that satisfies and delights. Each chapter begins with a question to help you define your present situation and determine where your secret choices have been taking you. The suggestions for action in each chapter will help you apply the material to your life and marriage. Remember, the more deeply you become involved, the more benefits you can enjoy.

Recognize, however, that you won't be able to do it all, or to do it all at once. These chapters are packed with good ideas and valuable principles from Scripture.

You'll be delighted with the results if you begin now and simply do what you can—every day. Be consistent, be expectant, and relax in the Lord's readiness to help you. This process offers hope, not more burdens to bear, so enjoy the experience, and remember the Lord's tender word of commendation: "She has done what she could" (Mark 14:8).

If you are pouring yourself into this study of secret choices to win your partner back or to restore a love that shows few signs of life, remember that the awakening and flowering of love cannot be forced. Make the right choices consistently, keep them "watered" with prayer, and wait for the results as patiently as possible. Good choices have a way of producing good fruit.

PART ONE

WHERE ARE YOUR CHOICES

TAKING YOU?

1
HARNESSING THE POWER

> Are we aware of our secret choices and their
> power in our lives?

*Choice: The voluntary act of selecting from two or more
things that which is preferred.*

When the alarm went off at 6 A.M., Mary Lou opened
her eyes, then sank back into sleep. Her husband Bill
made his breakfast and ate alone. Mary Lou felt rather
badly about it, but the choice was simplified several
mornings later when she didn't even hear the alarm. Bill
began going to the Doughnut Shop for breakfast and
companionship where an attractive waitress provided
both.

Bill and Mary Lou had established the habit of
exchanging kisses and hugs whenever one of them left
the house. But Bill, miffed at Mary Lou's failure to get
up for breakfast with him, decided one morning to
leave without her sleep-fogged kiss. Mary Lou, hurt

when she realized what he had done, retaliated by ignoring him that evening. Both were out of sorts at bedtime and turned their backs on one another instead of exchanging good-night hugs.

No major decisions here but a link-up of choices which are affecting this marriage. Life is a series of choices, most of them so small we scarcely realize that we're making them. Or why. Sometimes we call them *reactions* and disclaim any responsibility for them, not recognizing that reactions are choices, too. Not only are we often unaware of our choices, but we seldom give thought to where they are taking us and whether we want to go there. Though our choices are small when counted one at a time, their cumulative effect is more powerful than we can imagine. In reality, these private choices direct our steps, determine our behavior, change the quality of our relationships, and in the end, shape our lives.

To help you focus on your choices in marriage, we have a series of questions for you to consider in the privacy of your own heart. Each section of the book will pose new questions which we believe are crucial to your happiness and the health of your marriage. The first one is this: *Where are your choices taking you?* Or, more specifically, *Are your secret choices moving you in a positive direction toward a successful marriage?*

The point is **They can!** Our goal is to show you how.

> Become aware of your secret choices and discover their power in your life. This is the first step toward harnessing that power to build the marriage of your hopes and dreams.

Start by defining and describing where you want to go with your marriage. If you don't know where you're going, almost any road will do, but to harness the power of your secret choices, you must know precisely where you're headed and how to get there. We encourage you to begin now to develop a strong mental picture of your "destination" — the marriage you consider *successful* because it's the kind of marriage you and your partner desire.

Think about it. What comes to mind when you hear the phrase "a successful marriage"?

For most of us, this depends on whether we're describing someone else's marriage or our own. When it comes to other people, we're likely to measure success by how long they've been married, how well their children and grandchildren have turned out, and if they're still talking to one another after thirty or forty years.

But when it comes to our own marriage, we expect infinitely more, and the passing of time has little to do with our calculations. We want a great marriage *now* — whether "now" is three days after the ceremony, or two years and two children later. Success, we rightly feel, should be enjoyed today, not deferred until our Golden Wedding Anniversary.

And yet, impatience is not the way to a great marriage. It can take us on side roads and rocky detours that we'd rather avoid. Some people today are so impatient for instant success that they throw in the towel if the marriage doesn't feel good and work well from Day One! Unfortunately, these people will never know what happiness they missed out on: they can only wonder.

To create a beautiful marriage that fulfills God's

design and meets the deepest needs and desires of our hearts will take time. It is never a fortunate accident, but always an achievement — a work of art. Still, we don't have to wait for success. We can enjoy success all along the way, if we're moving in the right direction. The process of building a good marriage offers moment-by-moment rewards in love, enjoyment, and satisfaction. If you are going through this book with your partner, make it an experience you'll remember with pleasure for years to come. Take advantage of the opportunities for personal growth while you share the fun of turning your dreams into goals which you can attain by working together. Even if you are reading this book alone, your mate can share in the benefits and blessings as you make positive choices concerning your marriage.

What do people expect from their own marriage? Our conversations with hundreds of couples indicate that most people want to be loved, understood, and cared for by their marriage partner. To put it simply, they want their needs met!

Call this the *happiness factor*, for marital happiness usually reflects the degree to which husbands and wives can relate as intimate friends and lovers. This clearly is the first dimension of a successful marriage. To determine how well our own marriage is working in this dimension, we can ask ourselves: Do we know how to love each other? Do we feel loved? Do we take care of each other, meeting the other's needs freely and without complaint? Are we able to be close without holding anything back? Are we growing in intimacy day by day?

It's worth noting that men and women tend to use different standards in answering these questions, and they judge their relationship in highly subjective ways. However you measure it, the dimension of love and intimacy cannot be regarded as an optional feature. Look into the heart of any happy marriage and you will find exchanges of love and nurturing in an emotional climate where intimacy grows and thrives.

Second, we can measure success in our marriage by evaluating how well we get along as partners. Call this the *contentment factor,* for our ease of mind greatly depends on whether we can function as a good team in the arena of life. Is our partnership reasonably efficient and generally free from bickering, recriminations, and attempts to control one another? Do we agree on most things or adapt and compromise when necessary? Do we complement one another, each contributing to the success of our joint efforts? Can we depend on one another? Are we satisfied with the way our lives are going, (our finances, our social life, our careers, our home setting, our schedules, our in-law relationships, our family planning and rearing of children, and the like)? Do we derive real pleasure from sharing our lives, and working toward long-range goals together? A satisfying partnership is the second dimension of a successful marriage.

The third measure of success reaches far beyond the emotional pleasures of being loved or the practical contentment of sharing life with a good partner. This dimension connects us on the deepest level and provides us with our *purpose* for living as well as our most valuable *resources* for living. Let's call it *the strength and stability factor*. We all have a built-in need for an active belief system which provides joy, purpose, unity, coherence, and a strong sense of meaning for our lives.

Do we share this in our marriage? Are we bonded together by something greater than ourselves? Does our relationship have spiritual dimensions and powerful spiritual resources because we worship and serve God together? A marriage without this shared *reason for being* will, at best, be painfully incomplete.

When couples say "I do," they usually begin with the conviction that marriage will make things easier for them as well as happier because the sorrows as well as the joys of life can be shared. "Double the joy and half the sorrow" — that's the arithmetic of our expectations. The danger is that in such cases we expect our partner to do for us what only God can do. Without spiritual resources, we may disappoint one another badly. Our relationship may become "double the sorrow and half the joy," instead. But when God is at the center of our marriage, He can work in both of us, relieving our burdens of grief and anxiety so that we are free from the weight of them, filling the empty spots, refreshing our spirits, helping us to help each other, and blessing us with an ever-deepening oneness in Him.

To review, here are the dimensions of a successful marriage which can safely be followed in mapping out your own destination. Within the scope of this broad outline, begin to fill in the specific details of the marriage you and your partner desire.

The Three Dimensions of a Successful Marriage
1. An emotional climate of love and nurturing, with a growing intimacy;
2. The creation of a smooth-working, satisfying partnership;
3. A shared faith which provides meaning, direction, and unified purpose for your marriage, and spiritual resources for all your needs.

Always remember how important it is to keep the picture of the marriage you want fresh in your mind. As desirable goals fill your thoughts, you will find yourself making positive choices with more ease, and these choices will steer you steadily in the right direction. Besides that, as your marriage gets better and better, think how much both of you will enjoy the journey.

> Establish the picture of the marriage you desire, fill in the details, and keep it fresh in your mind to guide your choices. This is the second step in harnessing your secret choices to build a satisfying marriage.

SUGGESTIONS

1. Set up a large looseleaf notebook labeled *Choices*, which you can use for your own journey as you build the marriage of your hopes and dreams. Put sections in the notebook corresponding to the outline on the Contents page. (Note that Parts II, III, and IV correspond to the three dimensions of the successful marriage.) Make a practice of inserting helpful clippings, notes, and journal entries in the places where they are applicable. Keep your input positive! This will become your private resource book and a source of encouragement.

2. Write a journal entry answering the question in Part 1: *Where Are Your Choices Taking You in Your Marriage?* Base it on your past performance. Then record changes you expect to see as you learn to make choices that lead to success. Again, be patient!

3. If you own our new-marriage handbook, *The First Years of Forever,* or if you can borrow a copy,

study the handbooks for husband and wife (chapters 8 and 9). These chapters explain the seven basic ways to love your wife and the seven basic ways to respond to your husband. Make notes on these ways of loving and responding in marriage and enter them in the appropriate sections of your notebook.

2
WHO'S AT THE CONTROLS?

Have we learned how to take charge of our choices?

The last of human freedoms is the ability to choose one's attitude.

Viktor Frankl,
a concentration camp survivor

Every successful marriage depends on the ability of both partners to make good choices. Analyze even one enjoyable day spent together as husband and wife, and you'll see that it happened because both of you chose to respond rightly. Was it a pleasant surprise? Or do you consistently choose the best for your marriage? In other words, *have you learned how to take charge of your choices?*

To answer this question, it's necessary to focus on *the real you*, the part of you that weighs thoughts, feelings, and beliefs, and then chooses attitudes and actions.

Granted, this can be perplexing. Human behavior seems to be a hopeless tangle of complexities and contradictions, with an endless line of "experts" on the subject, each putting forth his or her own theories. Which one is right? Who knows? Sometimes we wonder if we will ever understand ourselves!

Fortunately, there is one authoritative book that understands us: the Bible. Recognizing that the Author of this book is the one who created us and knows us thoroughly, we can approach its contents with a thirst to know ourselves and the confidence that what we discover will be the truth and totally dependable.

When we begin in Genesis, we find that God created us with an amazing capacity to make our own choices. Amazing, because *willpower* is power indeed. This independent self called the will sits in the place of personal authority and responsibility, with power to decide and control even the most essential matters of faith and life.

If we were designing a world of new beings, would we allow that? Wouldn't we install built-in safeguards to make sure, at the very least, that our creatures recognized our superior position as Maker.

God, instead, made a world of men and women in His own image with the freedom *to choose* whether or not to love Him. He created us in His image as rational, morally aware, and morally responsible human beings — a fact with great relevance for us personally. It means that we must make our own choices, and live with the consequences.

This is a fact we tend to ignore or overlook. Too often, we forget that every choice has its consequences, or we try to escape those consequences by saying, "Don't blame me. It's not my fault. It's just the way I am." Or, "Someone else is to blame!"

This tendency to try to escape the consequences of our actions had its beginning at the time Adam and Eve made their disastrous choice to reject God's will in favor of their own. In that terrible moment when they had to explain their behavior and face the consequences of what they had done, the man, in effect, complained: "It was the woman's fault. She gave me the fruit to eat. And it was your fault, Lord, because you gave me the woman to be with me, and look what happened." The woman could only blame the serpent: "Lord, I was tricked! I was deceived by that serpent."

God responded by telling each of them, beginning with the serpent, the consequences of their actions: "Because you have done this . . . I will. . . ." The aftershocks of their choice go on and on, and we all suffer from the results. Our will has been so adversely affected that we not only find it hard to *do right,* but we find it hard *to choose to do right,* even when it is to our clear advantage.

Because our first ancestors rebelled at God's gracious design for their lives, that same rebellion has now spilled over into our own minds. The control center within us, which was meant to be in charge, is under attack on all fronts. We're besieged by our emotions, threatened by our fears, tricked by our lusts, lied to by the enemy of our souls (who promises that sin will bring us peace and pleasures), and sabotaged by outside influences which can do us no good.

This is why the question, "Who's at the controls?" is such an important one for the person who wants to build a good marriage. Such a marriage won't happen automatically, and it can't, because our control center cannot be depended upon to make good choices without some essential adjustments.

These adjustments become possible only when we are ready to accept responsibility for our choices, large or small, and the consequences which inevitably follow. Yes, God has given us the freedom we crave. Because of the way He created us, we are still free, even in the most oppressive conditions of a concentration camp or a Vietnam POW camp, to choose our beliefs and attitudes. But freedom costs because it makes us responsible.

> Remember that *every choice has its consequences,* and learn to "count the cost" before you act or react. This is the third step in your journey toward the marriage you desire.

Now, let's consider how the process of taking charge of our choices works. On the surface this appears to be a major attempt at self-improvement in which we stop taking the line of least resistance and start managing our life more constructively. Taking charge in this way sounds brisk, decisive, and invigorating, like an October football game. The crunch comes when we find that our self-efforts do not have the clout we expected.

In fact, almost from the moment we try to exert control and make improvements in the ways we think and behave, we find ourselves in a civil war, and the hopes of winning seem slim indeed. On the battlefield of our mind we face a dizzying array of enemies and obstacles. We have already mentioned a few: fears, lusts, and selfish desires, emotions threatening to take control, temptations, deceptions, distractions, doubts, confusions, pressures from outside, and a disturbing inability to operate decisively, no matter how hard we try. Naturally, in most cases, the white flag goes up.

If we can't control our choices, what's the point of writing a book about them? This is a fair question. The Scriptures supply the best of answers: God, who gave us our human will with its power to choose, has not left us helpless before our enemies, whether within or without. The Bible assures us of this in many ways. Here it is put most plainly:

> He Himself has said, "I will never desert you, nor will I ever forsake you" (Heb. 13:5b NASB).

The word "forsake" is a compound of three Greek words meaning, *leave behind in*. He is not going to leave us behind in this battle of our mind and will. As we will see, He has a solution! Another translation of the same verse says,

> I will in no wise desert you or leave you alone on the field of conquest or in a position of suffering. I will in no wise let go, loose hold my sustaining grasp (Westcott).

God has committed Himself to helping us. Because He has the loving-kindness to do this for us and the authority and power to accomplish it, we *can* take charge of our choices through His energizing and by His guidance. "Thanks be to God, who gives us the victory through our Lord Jesus Christ" (1 Cor. 15:57 NASB)!

The New Testament gives the wonderful details of this victory which can exert such a life-changing effect on us. It becomes the absorbing study of a lifetime for those who trust in Him and learn to experience His victory in various areas of their life. In this book we want to concentrate on one area, the choice-making process. Because of God's provision, we can make good choices, stick with them, and live them out in our marriage — not by self-effort, but by linking our willpower (our willingness to behave responsibly) with God's enabling, indwelling power. All the other counsel we have for you depends on this point first.

> Understand this basic principle: *Your willingness to behave responsibly needs to be coupled with God's power.* This is the fourth step in your quest for a fulfilling marriage.

Because all of God's provisions, including His infusion of power and ability, come to us through *salvation*, we must begin there. This is the essential adjustment which makes it possible for us to function as we were originally designed to. If you have not put your trust in Jesus Christ (and this is a very personal matter which only you can determine), please turn at once to chapter 14 for information on how to "choose life," that first and most important decision which will set you free to choose all other good things, including the best possible marriage.

As soon as your personal relationship with the Lord

Jesus Christ is established, you can begin to discover the meaning of this important counsel for your life:

> Work out your own salvation with fear and trembling. For it is God which worketh in you both to will and to do of *his* good pleasure (Phil. 2:12b, 13 KJV).

We do not work *for* our salvation: that is a free gift. Instead, we "work out" the salvation He has put within us, expressing what God has given us by His Spirit; putting it into practice in our daily living through our actions, words, and attitudes. We are counseled to do this with a sense of awe and responsibility. And as we live responsibly, we have the assurance that God is continually at work within us, giving us both the will to choose and the power to achieve those things which God knows are best for us.

How do we learn what is God's best for us? By consistently referring to the Bible as our guidebook for daily living. As we do this, God is able to direct us and change us by renewing our mind and replacing old, harmful ways of thinking with a fresh, biblical viewpoint which will bless us as individuals and benefit our marriage beyond description.

> Do not conform any longer to the pattern of this world, but be transformed by the renewing of your mind. Then you will be able to test and approve what God's will is — his good, pleasing and perfect will (Rom. 12:2).

In other words, don't allow the world around you to press you into its mold, because God has something much better for you. He wants to transform you! (The Greek verb for transform is the word from which we get our English word *metamorphosis*.)

He's talking about a total change from the inside out, and it is an ongoing process. "Keep on being transformed . . ." the Greek New Testament says.

The key to this change is always our mind, the control center of our thoughts, feelings, actions, attitudes, and beliefs. God, through His indwelling Spirit, can and will make it new again, as we keep the truth of His Word flowing through our mind while maintaining the vital connections of prayer and Christian fellowship. If we allow Him to do so (for we always have the power of choice), He quietly changes our thinking and attitudes, and we discover by experience that His will for us is always good and wonderful — the best thing and the safest thing that could happen to us. As we grow in this confidence, we begin to choose and desire His will above everything else, and in the end we find His promise true:

> Delight thyself also in the Lord; and he shall give thee the desires of thine heart. Commit thy way unto the Lord; trust also in him, and he shall bring *it* to pass (Ps. 37:4 – 5 KJV).

When we discover that God's will for us is better than our own choices, we also learn to trust Him concerning the caution signs and the red flag warnings He gives us in the Scriptures. His way is to tell us the consequences of certain actions and attitudes — the unpleasant cause and effect of our self-willed choices. We learn to believe Him, for as we grow to know Him, we learn that He is Love, and that His intentions toward us are always *good*.

His concise counsel for us in making and implementing choices can be found in the fourth chapter of Ephesians, verses 22 – 24:

> (1) . . . put off your old self, which is being corrupted by its deceitful desires;
> (2) . . . be made new in the attitude of your minds;
> (3) . . . put on the new self, created to be like God in true righteousness and holiness.

The choice to do this must be ours; the power, His. "I can do everything through him who gives me strength" (Phil. 4:13). Who's at the controls? Note that the *I* remains, but not the old self-will. You cannot operate the controls effectively by your own power; neither can the Lord do it without your cooperation in choosing to listen to Him and follow His instructions. A teacher of the Word has observed that the secret of power is to discover and to learn from the New Testament *what is possible for us in Christ.* God has never counseled us to do something impossible! Instead, the responsibility we emphasized earlier in this chapter can become what Jay E. Adams has called *respond ability:* the God-given ability to respond as God says man and woman should respond to every situation of life.

The remainder of this book will present you with specific choices that can determine the quality of your marriage, along with other options and their predictable consequences. We have found that the most helpful marriage counseling always emphasizes God's pattern for relating as husband and wife, and we pray that this will become the standard which guides your major decisions and every secret choice.

Keep your mind renewed with the Word of
God so that you can learn how to respond in
every situation of marriage according to His
good counsel. This is the fifth step in building a
love-filled, lasting marriage.

SUGGESTIONS

1. In your notebook record some ways you chose
to react to your partner this week and note the immediate results of that choice. Then describe a more positive
choice you could have made and the probable results.
How does this fit in with your picture of a successful
marriage?

2. Describe some difficulties you have had in
choosing to do right, or following through on your
choices. Then write about a special time when you
know you experienced God's help and guidance in
making a good choice and sticking with it. If you want
His power and direction in your marriage, express your
longing in the form of a poem, a prayer, or a letter to
the Lord.

3. Take the outline in Ephesians 4:22 – 24, and set
some personal goals concerning what you want to "put
off," what you want to "put on," and new attitudes you
would like God to renew in your mind. See if you can
find Bible verses which give guidance related to the
subject matter of the goals you have set. Meditate on
them "day and night," and see what happens!

4. Read Psalm 1 every day until it becomes a part
of you.

3
CONSULTING THE MARRIAGE MAP

Are we patterning our marriage after the
Creator's original design for our happiness?

*Through skillful and godly Wisdom is a house (a life,
a home, a family) built, and by understanding it is
established (on a sound and good foundation). And
by its knowledge shall the chambers (of its every
area) be filled with all precious and pleasant riches
(Prov. 24:3 – 4 AMPLIFIED).*

In the first chapter, we encouraged you to develop a
strong mental picture of the marriage you desire so that
you could harness your secret choices to move in that
direction. Now, if you have your "destination" in view,
it's time to consult the marriage map — the Bible,
which reveals God's perfect design for marriage.

In its pages, from Genesis to Revelation, you can find
what you need to build a marriage which will bring lasting happiness because it follows God's original design.

This design is conveyed to us in the form of basic principles, specific instructions, clear guidelines, vivid examples, sobering warnings, and wise counsel. Nothing can take the place of God's wisdom in showing you how to build your house — your life, your home, and your family — to last a lifetime, and how to fill every room of your life together with "all precious and pleasant riches."

Although we can't communicate all of this in a single chapter, we can make a survey of God's wisdom on marriage which will show you what God considers most important in your relationship. After all, He created marriage for our blessing, and He knows best how to make it work!

We asked you to define a successful marriage from your perspective. Now, we need to go to the Scriptures to answer the same question from the divine viewpoint. Keep in mind that Paul, in the book of Ephesians, called marriage "a great mystery." *Mystery* in the New Testament usually refers to something we could never solve by ourselves — a secret which God has now revealed to us. Let's explore this mystery together in the light of God's revelations about marriage.

THE MEANING OF MARRIAGE

To look into the meaning of marriage, we need to return to the first wedding (a garden wedding!) where it all began.

> And the Lord God caused a deep sleep to fall upon Adam, and he slept: and he took one of his ribs, and closed up the flesh instead thereof;

> And the rib, which the Lord God had taken from man, made he a woman, and brought her unto the man.
>
> And Adam said, This is now bone of my bones, and flesh of my flesh: she shall be called Woman, because she was taken out of Man.
>
> Therefore shall a man leave his father and his mother, and shall cleave unto his wife: and they shall be one flesh.
>
> And they were both naked, the man and his wife, and were not ashamed (Gen. 2:21 – 25 KJV).

This was the first marriage ceremony: *Made he a woman, and brought her to the man.* God made the woman to complement Adam perfectly, as an artist producing a masterpiece. That is what the original language conveys. Please note that the initiative in marriage, the plan, the design, and the creation of the two human beings for each other — together reflecting the image of God, and yet separately incomplete — began and remains under the watchful care of the Lord God. Marriage is not something devised by a blundering man, full of flaws and bugs needing to be worked out. God's way with a man and a woman in marriage is perfect and beautiful, and His plan is still in effect today.

At this first wedding, the bridegroom provided the special music. His song, *Bone of my bones and flesh of my flesh,* suggests another aspect of the mystery of marriage: the kinship we feel with our mate while still retaining our individuality.

In a sense, we, too, share Adam's experience: we survey the other creatures of the world, finding no one quite right for us, and then God brings us to the one person with whom we feel akin. Even though we may be very unlike one another, yet we know we are closer than blood relatives, as close in heart and being as though we shared bones and flesh. We know within our spirits that *we belong!* God designed this mystery of marriage to heal our loneliness.

At weddings, the music (such as Adam sang) usually provides a lovely prelude to the promises made by the couple, promises so sacred we call them wedding vows. In the perfection of the Garden, where man and woman knew only good, vows were unnecessary. Instead, God taught Adam the terms of the marriage covenant He had established for the human race. The terms have never been revised or replaced, and still provide the most concise and most effective marriage counsel ever given:

> *Leave all else,* giving your primary and whole-hearted loyalty and attention to one another;
>
> *Cleave to one another* until you become inseparable, coming together in spirit so completely that you are one and the seam can no longer be found;
>
> *Become one flesh,* with your oneness of heart, spirit, and shared life symbolized by and expressed through sexual union.

As we consider this three-part counsel we can see that marriage rests on two pillars which are far more than ornamental. They are *oneness* and *permanence*. God really does expect husband and wife to become *one* and to continue growing in oneness over the course of a lifetime. But the benefits of marriage can bless us only in the context of permanence. Temporary oneness would bring harm, not blessing. If we are to be one with our mate, it must be within a permanent relationship.

We need to *leave* all else, for other pulls must give up their power; we can only know oneness with one person. Even our children, dear though they are to us, must be excluded from the center of this relationship, for we are not one with our offspring; only with our mate. Leaving prepares us for oneness. Cleaving establishes the fact of permanence in our minds and reassures our hearts that we *are* loved and *shall* be loved tomorrow.

After the wedding comes the honeymoon. In the case of Adam and Eve, it was a perfect honeymoon, for in the sunlit and star-bathed delights of marriage in the Garden, both were naked and were not ashamed. No barriers existed between them: there was nothing to hide, nothing to overcome. What liberty of mind, body, and spirit they must have experienced — liberty to love and become one, without the conflicts which tear at us while we painfully learn our lessons in oneness.

Earlier in this book, we referred to the sad aftermath of the Garden wedding. You can read in the third chapter of Genesis how the man and woman failed to obey God in their ideal environment; how they fell from a state of innocence into sin and death; and how God promised redemption and expelled the couple from the Garden of Eden to live a life of moral responsibility under new and difficult conditions. The oneness of the man and woman could no longer be assumed and enjoyed without effort.

Their unity broken, Adam and Eve's relationship became separate and selfish, their love contaminated with hostility and blame. And so, today, we still cope with sin, shame, selfishness, self-centeredness, and separateness. We all have the tendency to withdraw from one another, to concentrate on our own needs and wants, to live for ourselves, and to blame those closest to us when things do not go as we desire.

As an indication of the influence of Genesis 3 on today's society, listen to this wife's words concerning her marital problems.

> "When I married Jeff, I meant it to be forever, but now I'm seriously considering a divorce. A few months ago I began having an affair with a man I met at work. He has invited me to move in with him — and I haven't decided to do that yet, but this affair has made me question whether Jeff and I can ever be happy together."

Her story is ordinary enough by today's standards, yet incredibly off the mark when compared to the Genesis marriage covenant.

Someone may ask, "Does God really expect people in today's world to live out a marriage ordinance that was given in the perfect environment of the Garden? How can His original plan still work in a world alienated by sin? Hasn't He somehow revised His marriage plan to fit prevailing conditions?"

*   *   *

THE QUESTION OF DIVORCE

This may be one of the most important questions you can ever ask, and it's essential to get the right answer firmly implanted in your understanding. The biblical marriage map can guide you only so far without this truth straight from the lips of the Lord Jesus Christ. In Mark 10:2 – 12 and in the parallel passage in Matthew 19:3 – 12, Jesus communicates the divine viewpoint of marriage. Listen for truth in a pure form, untarnished by the hardness of people's hearts:

> And the Pharisees came to him, and asked him, Is it lawful for a man to put away *his* wife? tempting him.
>
> And he answered and said unto them, What did Moses command you?
>
> And they said, Moses suffered to write a bill of divorcement, and to put her away.
>
> And Jesus answered and said unto them, For the hardness of your heart he wrote you this precept.
>
> But from the beginning of the creation God made them male and female.
>
> For this cause shall a man leave his father and mother, and cleave to his wife;
>
> And they twain shall be one flesh: so then they are no more twain, but one flesh.
>
> What therefore God hath joined together, let not man put asunder.

And in the house his disciples asked him again of
the same *matter*.

And he saith unto them, Whosoever shall put
away his wife, and marry another, committeth
adultery against her.

And if a woman shall put away her husband, and
be married to another, she committeth adultery
(Mark 10:2 – 12 KJV).

If we want to know what our own attitude toward
marriage and divorce should be today, we can learn from
Jesus' response to the Pharisees. He ignored the bickering
"religious" authorities of the day and their preoccupation
with excuses for divorce; He focused on the Scriptures as
the only real authority; and He went back to the original
design for marriage in the Genesis account as the only
relevant topic of discussion. Matthew records that Jesus
first answered the Pharisees this way: "Haven't you even
read Genesis 1:27 and 2:24, you people who are always
boasting about your knowledge of the Scriptures?" In
other words, "Why don't you go to the original teaching
on marriage to find your answers?"

Jesus recognized these two Genesis passages as the
divine ordinance for marriage which remains very
much in effect in a sin-marred world. He made it clear
that Moses' concession for the hardness of men's hearts
was not the issue for anyone who really wanted to
understand God's plan and purpose for marriage.
"From the beginning it was not so," He said in Matthew
19:8, directing us back to the beginning where we still
find our instructions for marriage and the standards we
need to follow.

He did add one new statement to the Genesis ordinance: *"What therefore God hath joined together, let not man put asunder"* (Matt. 19:6; Mark 10:9). When a man and woman marry, God participates in yoking them together, changing what has been two into one. From the divine viewpoint, marriage is a union which all the courts of the land cannot dissolve.

What does this mean to you today? It means that even admitting the possibility of divorce can adversely affect the development of your love relationship. Retaining the idea of divorce in your emotional vocabulary can actually sabotage your attempts to grow in love and oneness, and keeping divorce as an escape clause suggests a flaw in your commitment which may become fatal at some point.

We realize that some of you have remarried after an unhappy first marriage and subsequent divorce.

Please keep this truth in view: God can take us where we are at any given moment and work out His plan for our life. If there are mistakes in your past concerning marriage and divorce, ask God's forgiveness and receive it, knowing that you have been set free from guilt. He always deals with us in the now, and you have every opportunity to go forward in a new way, conforming your new marriage to His original design.

THE BENEFITS OF MARRIAGE

But what are the purposes behind this design? What benefits did God have in mind for us? Let's consider the scriptural evidence. The blessings of marriage seem to

fall into three main categories which we have listed
below along with Scriptures which can help you understand the way God sees your marriage relationship, and
the potential it holds for your happiness. Note that
these categories correspond to the three dimensions of
marriage which we described in chapter 1: the emotional climate of love, nurturing, and intimacy; the satisfying partnership; and the spiritual dimensions and
purposes of marriage.

1. *Marriage was designed to provide the security of a
"house of love" for the enjoyment of romantic fulfillment,
intimate friendship, and sexual delights in the permanent
setting of a steadfast covenant relationship.*

> My lover spoke and said to me, "Arise, my darling,
> my beautiful one, and come with me." . . . He has
> taken me to the banquet hall, and his banner over
> me was love. . . . Place me like a seal over your
> heart . . . for love is as strong as death. . . . It burns
> like blazing fire, like a mighty flame. Many waters
> cannot quench love; rivers cannot wash it away. . . .
> (Song 2:10, 4; 8:6, 7).

> May you rejoice in the wife of your youth. A lov-
> ing doe, a graceful deer — may her breasts satisfy
> you always, may you ever be captivated by her
> love. Why be captivated, my son, by an adulter-
> ess? Why embrace the bosom of another man's
> wife? (Prov. 5:18 – 20).

> You flood the Lord's altar with tears. You weep
> and wail because he no longer pays attention to
> your offerings or accepts them with pleasure from

your hands. You ask, "Why?" It is because the
Lord is acting as the witness between you and the
wife of your youth, because you have broken faith
with her, though she is your partner, the wife of
your marriage covenant. . . . So guard yourself in
your spirit, and do not break faith with the wife of
your youth. "I hate divorce," says the Lord God of
Israel (Mal. 2:13 – 16).

2. *Marriage was designed to heal man and woman's alone-
ness, to provide a suitable helper, friend, and ally to sus-
tain and support the other in the challenges of daily living,
and to encourage one another in following and serving the
Lord.*

The Lord God said, "It is not good for the man to
be alone. I will make a helper suitable for him"
(Gen. 2:18).

A wife of noble character who can find? She is
worth far more than rubies. Her husband has full
confidence in her and lacks nothing of value. She
brings him good, not harm, all the days of her life
(Prov. 31:10 – 11).

Two are better than one, because they have a good
return for their work: If one falls down, his friend
can help him up. But pity the man who falls and
has no one to help him up! Also, if two lie down
together, they will keep warm. But how can one
keep warm alone? Though one may be overpow-
ered, two can defend themselves. A cord of three
strands is not quickly broken (Eccl. 4:9 – 12).

3. Marriage was designed to picture the relationship of Jesus Christ and His church — the oneness, sacrificial love, and submission — and to give an example of heaven on earth to a watching world. It is also the place in which to produce and rear godly families in this setting of love, and to train them to serve the Lord.

So God created man in his own image, in the image of God he created him; male and female he created them. God blessed them and said to them, "Be fruitful and increase in number; fill the earth and subdue it" (Gen. 1:27 – 28).

"Choose for yourselves this day whom you will serve. . . . But as for me and my household, we will serve the Lord " (Josh. 24:15).

Love the Lord your God with all your heart and with all your soul and with all your strength. These commandments that I give you today are to be upon your hearts. Impress them on your children. Talk about them when you sit at home and when you walk along the road. . . . Write them on the doorframes of your houses and on your gates (Deut. 6:5 – 7, 9).

Has not the Lord made them one? In flesh and spirit they are his. And why one? Because he was seeking godly offspring. So guard yourself in your spirit, and do not break faith with the wife of your youth (Mal. 2:15).

Submit to one another out of reverence for Christ. Wives, submit to your husbands as to the Lord. For the husband is the head of the wife as Christ is the head of the church, his body, of which he is the Savior. Now as the church submits to Christ, so also wives should submit to their husbands in everything. Husbands, love your wives, just as Christ loved the church and gave himself up for her to make her holy, cleansing her by the washing with water through the word, and to present her to himself as a radiant church, without stain or wrinkle or any other blemish, but holy and blameless. In this same way, husbands ought to love their wives as their own bodies. He who loves his wife loves himself. After all, no one ever hated his own body, but he feeds and cares for it, just as Christ does the church. . . . "For this reason a man will leave his father and mother and be united to his wife, and the two will become one flesh." This is a profound mystery — but I am talking about Christ and the church. However, each one of you also must love his wife as he loves himself, and the wife must respect her husband.

Children, obey your parents in the Lord, for this is right. "Honor your father and mother" — which is the first commandment with a promise — "that it may go well with you and that you may enjoy long life on the earth."

Fathers, do not exasperate your children; instead, bring them up in the training and instruction of the Lord (Eph. 5:21 – 33; 6:1 – 4).

CHECKLIST FOR A GOOD MARRIAGE

Here's a look at the marriage map of the Bible from another perspective. Use these nine scriptural characteristics of a good marriage as a checklist and a basis for making your choices:

1. Both partners have left their parents to establish their own independent family unit. Neither is unduly influenced by their families and neither is emotionally bound to them.

2. Partners are cleaving to one another so that nothing on earth is as important to them as their mate and their marriage.

3. They are growing in physical, emotional, and spiritual oneness which includes Bible reading, prayer, and church participation.

4. They are enjoying the delights of romantic love.

5. They have a strong view of the permanence of marriage and a steadfast faithfulness to one another.

6. They help each other in all the details of living.

7. They meet each other's needs and forgive each other freely so that they no longer feel alone.

8. They relate in mutual love and submission, learning how to love one another by studying the relationship of Jesus Christ and His church.

9. Their marriage becomes a house of love so that it offers the right setting to rear and nurture children; to minister to others in need of love and encouragement; and to portray to the world something of the love which Jesus Christ has for His people to become "a showcase for heaven."

Set against these wonderful benefits of marriage are the misunderstandings and false conceptions of marriage

which influence many minds today. Check the chart we
have prepared to contrast the two views of marriage,
and be alert to these subtle lies which can so easily
shape our thinking before we realize what has happened to us.

MARRIAGE: TWO VIEWS

Human Perspective	Divine Perspective
Self-Centered	"Two Become One"
"I" Mentality	"We" Mentality
Temporary	Permanent
Conditional Partnership	Indissoluble Union
"An Experience"	A Lifetime Covenant
"As long as I like it"	Commitment—"No matter what"
"I'll try . . ."	"I Do!"
"Unless I fall in love with someone else"	"Till Death Do Us Part"
No direction or meaning	Purposeful, following God's Design
"Divorce is always an option."	"What God has joined let not man put asunder."
"I have to decide what's best for me."	"Love means doing the best for my partner."
Separateness	Togetherness

One writer has said that marriage, essentially,
involves a lifelong commitment to do a good, thorough
job of loving one person.

We agree. But this requires work! The mingling of
identities, the maintaining of a binding covenant, and
the nurturing of a love affair through all the wild

clashes of self-assertion which a couple have to survive to find their way into the peaceful place of genuine one-ness takes consistent effort, time, and patience. It will help immensely if we hold ever fresh in our minds the picture of marriage as God has designed it, and what that can mean in our life.

> Study the Creator's original design for mar-riage, and live by His design. This is the sixth step in building a good marriage.

SUGGESTIONS

1. Write three ways you need to change your behavior as a husband or wife based on biblical infor-mation in this chapter. Be very specific. Exercise your choices as described in chapter 2.

2. Analyze whether there are any differences between the marriage you desire and God's original marriage design. Comment on this in your notebook.

3. Read the Scriptures in this chapter aloud with your marriage partner as though this were a personal let-ter to you from the Lord. For daily devotions, divide the Scriptures up into a week's portions. Record thoughts shared by your partner and ideas for fulfilling the com-mands and examples.

PART TWO

WHAT KIND OF EMOTIONAL
CLIMATE ARE YOU CREATING?

4

DISTANCE OR INTIMACY

Are we moving closer or growing apart?

"This . . . my lover, this my friend" (Song of Songs 5:16).

As you begin Part 2, we have another crucial question for you: *What kind of emotional climate are you creating with your secret choices?* Is it an environment of love, nurturing, and intimacy? Or, distance, . . . neglect, . . . indifference?

Your first reaction may be to opt for a gray area somewhere in between. Couples sometimes answer, "Well, we're not doing all that great, but we're not doing so bad either. On a scale of one to ten, give us a five."

The truth is, you are continuing to move in one direction or the other, and at some point, however subtle the change, the scales will clearly shift to show what has been happening all along. Although you may not realize it, you are growing closer or drifting farther apart every day of your marriage. Even the smallest choice — whether to curl up next to your mate on the couch or plump down in a chair across the room — is taking you toward one of two opposing poles: emotional distance or intimacy.

Because of the demands of daily living, we can go for periods of time without realizing what is happening in our relationship. Sometimes we're not even aware of our secret choices because we assume ourselves to be something that we're not. We may pride ourselves on being the kind of marriage partner with a capacity for intimate closeness, but our actions communicate something quite different to our mate. We may describe ourselves as loving, nurturing individuals, but this has little effect on how we behave. Our will — which decides what will happen — has chosen otherwise, and our conduct reflects our true choice.

This is why we emphasize the adjective *secret* when speaking of the choices that determine the success of our marriage. These choices, which take us in one direction or the other, happen on the inside first. Afterward, because of subtle clues communicated through our behavior and attitudes, our husband or wife can sense that change is taking place on the inside, "where the meanings are." Still later, the results (positive or negative) can be seen by all.

When changes are perceived as negative, the question is, Have we changed, or is our partner beginning to know us as we really are? After all, dating affords the opportunity to put on our nicest face, our most agreeable personality, and our best behavior. When we live together twenty-four hours a day in the bonding of marriage, such well-meaning pretense is no longer possible. Under the glare of reality, unrealistic expectations can cause many a problem and forge major obstacles to the enjoyment of intimacy. Because you can only build a rewarding, intimate relationship with a person who is well known to you and lovingly understood and accepted, it's important to learn to relate to the one you actually married, not to the idealized person you dreamed of marrying.

In real life your "prince" may refuse to hold hands with you at the park. Your "princess" may criticize you and take your boss's side. Your lover may roll over and go to sleep instead of cuddling you in his arms for a good-night chat. Your sweetheart may watch TV until 2:00 A.M. when you want her to go to bed with you at 10:00. It may not be as bad as that, or it might be worse. Any genuine relationship which offers the "magic" of love also contains the seed of disappointments, flaws, and failures.

Few of us are aware of that reality at the beginning of marriage, for our expectations run high. When we meet the person who seems to fill in the lonely spaces in our heart, and the feeling is shared, we say it's too good to be true, but we believe that it is true anyhow! We desperately want to believe we have found the ideal love relationship which will fulfill all of our dreams. After marriage, when discontent slips in, when we discover that our partner is less than "a perfect fit" as a mate, and that our relationship is less than the perfection we counted on, this may disappoint us and disturb us, but it can also mark the beginning of our true love affair. Wisdom tells us that although life will not be a perpetual honeymoon, something much better, much richer, can be ours *if* we're willing to direct our secret choices toward building love-filled intimacy with the *real* person we married.

This means, of course, that we have to be real, too, and unafraid of revealing ourselves in an intimate relationship.

Nothing is more real than intimacy, and to build it in our marriage, we need to begin by converting our false assumptions about ourselves and our unrealistic expectations of our mate and marriage into reality-based thinking.

> See yourself and your partner as you really are, and love, accept, and delight in your partner on the basis of reality. This is the seventh step in establishing the kind of marriage that every couple needs.

Our goal in this chapter is to help you use your secret choices to develop that incomparable closeness of an intimate marriage in which you share the restful assurance that you are fully known and deeply loved. You may have had intimate friends who enriched your life, but this should surpass any other relationship, for intimacy in marriage is as close as two human beings can get. As the quote from the *Song of Songs* at the beginning of this chapter suggests, an intimate marriage involves two roles in combination: lover and best friend. Intimacy enjoyed in the security of marriage offers us the ultimate pleasures of life and, at the same time, heals our innermost loneliness as nothing else can.

To make the best choices for intimacy, it's necessary to grasp the key position of intimacy in a good marriage. This example from the world of architecture offers some interesting parallels. Picture a stone arch representing your love relationship. The stone looks strong enough, but in order to maintain its structure, this arch needs a keystone. Although the keystone is only one of a number of associated part, (just as intimacy is only one aspect of your relationship), it is the key element that holds the others together. It does this by causing the downward pressure on the arch to be evenly exerted throughout the whole structure.

The same thing happens when two people share everything in their lives through the experience of intimacy. All the pressures of life, bearing down on the marriage and on either or both of the partners, become evenly shared and their impact lessened by the presence of intimacy. Medical doctors have found that an intimate relationship between a husband and wife can determine how well that couple masters the crises of life. A high degree of intimacy can also provide shelter and relief from the ordinary tensions of life. Life becomes richer and more colorful when shared with an intimate partner; it offers love and laughter, pleasure and stability. In fact, we believe the secret of staying in love for any married couple can be summed up in this one potent word: *intimacy*.

Recall the picture of the arch: Its keystone fits into the top of the arch in the central position, strengthening the entire structure; at the same time it provides an ornamental touch. The keystone is seen by all, it's decorative, and it's essential! When thinking of the opportunities to build intimacy in your relationship, remember the lesson of the keystone.

Intimacy in marriage can be defined this way: **The intimate relationship of husband and wife is a deeply satisfying closeness of mind, heart, body, and spirit which is shared and experienced by two equals who relate as lovers and best friends in the permanent context of marriage.**

But keep in mind that marriage never guarantees the delights of intimacy. If you read the current magazines, you know that couples seem to have great difficulty achieving this intimacy. Yet they all expect it, and, without it, marriages often disintegrate. Even in stable marriages, couples sometimes admit to an emptiness at the core of their relationship because one or both do not know how to become intimate lovers or are afraid to try.

You can be the happy exception. Be assured that God desires you to have the best, and in a world of shifting relationships, the two of you *can* experience an ongoing, always growing intimacy which is so different from the norm that a world of lonely people will want to know your secret.

The secret involves understanding the inmost workings of an intimate relationship and then learning to make moment-by-moment choices based on your knowledge, like a good athlete making the right moves without conscious decisions because he or she has thought it all through ahead of time.

One thing is certain: You cannot create intimacy by making an intellectual choice to do it. You can love someone with unconditional love by the choice of your will and continue to do so, whether or not the person responds. But it takes two for intimacy, and response is its "life blood." How then can you use your secret choices to obtain intimacy? By doing those things which will enhance it, promote it, and give it room to grow. By providing an emotional climate which will nurture it in your marriage and *cause* it to grow.

Here are the guidelines we have found helpful in understanding intimacy and "growing it" in marriage.

TEN GUIDELINES FOR INTIMACY IN MARRIAGE

1. *Always remember that intimacy depends on the experience of shared feelings.*

Intimacy is experiential in nature. It is not perceived in the mind as something that *should* be there: It is felt instinctively and viscerally. You know intuitively — your feelings tell you — whether your intimacy is flourishing or fading. You *know* if something is wrong between you, and you feel relief the moment everything is all right again. In this private, most personal relationship, the two of you become so finely tuned to one another that you can be constantly alert and responsive to one another's fluctuations of feeling and well-being at any given moment.

This means that if you want emotional intimacy in your marriage, you will have to gain a good understanding of your partner's feelings. There is no shortcut for this. You will need to study your partner lovingly and *listen* to your partner with your whole being. Both of you will need to develop your verbal skills and learn how to talk about your inner life with one another. Intimacy can only come out of your free choice to know and be fully known in return — a choice each must make individually, for intimacy is a reciprocal process.

When people marry, each comes into the relationship with different habits formed in childhood concerning closeness and space; togetherness and privacy. It takes time and patient efforts to arrive at a comfort zone which both can accept. A person who has been raised to be "detached" from loved ones will have to learn by experience the delights of intimacy in marriage. Please do not allow this to become a matter of controversy in the meantime. When only one of you desires a more intimate relationship, you will need to set up the conditions whereby your partner also feels motivated to desire it. This, too, develops out of careful, loving study of your partner, and delicate pursuit over a period of time.

2. *Learn, by practice, to express your inner feelings to one another.*

In shallow relationships, not much exchange of information about inner selves takes place. By contrast, in a meaningful relationship, people reveal how they feel and why, sharing their personal history of sorrows, joys, accomplishments, disappointments, changes, and growth.

A common problem with this sharing is that the husband may find it difficult to talk about his feelings. It's been a long-held notion that women are more emotional than men, but this is only part truth, if truth at all. According to recent research, men and women respond emotionally to events with equal intensity. The real difference is that women are more able to describe their responses and reactions in emotional terms. Women can usually tell you what they're feeling at the moment. A man can talk about what's happening, but may have difficulty expressing how he feels about it.

An understanding wife will make it easier for her husband to talk about his feelings by patiently drawing him out, not by putting him down. If the experience of sharing becomes disagreeable, all is lost. One wife we know got her husband to start sharing his feelings by what she called "Sunday afternoon communication breaks." The two would lie across the bed, sharing thoughts, or go for a leisurely walk together. From sharing thoughts, she would move into sharing feelings, and exhibit such a gentle interest in her husband's feelings that he began to enjoy expressing them.

She says, "I've learned three things about this. First, don't prolong the sharing times. Men seem to get bored easily with this kind of talking, so be sensitive to signs of restlessness. Second, make the experience extremely pleasant for your husband. Third, communicate your genuine interest in knowing him better. Of course, he has to be sure this is all in the strictest confidence and that you'll never use it against him later. I see that it's not easy for men to become vulnerable to their wives. It takes a lot of trust — and practice, too."

The husband who wants his wife to fall in love with him utterly and completely will win her heart by following the example of the lover in the Song of Songs:

> O my dove, *that art* in the clefts of the rock, in the secret *places* of the stairs, let me see thy countenance, let me hear thy voice; for sweet is thy voice, and thy countenance *is* comely (Song 2:14 KJV).

What wife wouldn't be thrilled with a husband who wanted to get her alone *to talk with her,* to hear what she had to say to him? A wife is touched when a husband cares enough to ask, "What are you thinking right now?" because he really wants to know what she is thinking and feeling and desiring. This is characteristic of lovers, but husbands and wives sometimes forget that they ever were lovers, that this is how their marriage began! It's important for you to continue to relate as two people in love, sharing your feelings out of your desire for intimacy.

Is there a place for sharing negative feelings in an intimate relationship? Yes, all feelings need to be shared, but you must be careful to share them lovingly and tactfully.

Therapists believe that one of the greatest destructive elements in a relationship is the inability to relate what you're feeling at the moment, and to lapse into brooding silence, instead. Learning to name and share your feelings will not only promote intimacy, but will protect your marriage as well.

We encourage you to study the chapter on communication in our new-marriage handbook, *The First Years of Forever,* while you improve your skills by practice.

3. *Display a mutual respect for one another, a mutual hunger to know one another better, and a growing delight in one another.*

Intimacy develops between two respected equals who share their inner lives *because they want to,* because they have a vital interest in one another's thoughts and feelings. If one partner is seemingly not interested, the effect may be withdrawal on the other side too.

This wife's comment to us is typical, "I don't feel

that my husband is receptive to my emotional needs. I know this is why I have withdrawn from him, and, even when I want to, I can't share with him anymore."

Husbands may not realize what they are communicating to their wives by this apparent indifference. A few years ago a women's magazine carried a short feature on "How to Discourage an Unwanted Relationship." It was, of course, directed to the woman reader, but let's change the focus. Husband, if you want to convince your wife that you are not interested in an intimate relationship with her,

    1. don't listen to her.
    2. don't look at her.
    3. turn down her offers.
    4. figure out what she wants and offer the opposite.
    5. be in a hurry.
    6. be busy.
    7. never offer her any encouragement.
    8. be supercritical.
    9. bring up touchy subjects.
  10. say, "I don't have time for you."

The opposite also is true. If you want to convince your partner of your interest and your desire for more intimacy in your marriage,

    1. listen.
    2. look.
    3. respond to offers.
    4. figure out what your mate wants and offer it.
    5. never be in a hurry when your presence is desired.
    6. don't be too busy for your mate.

7. encourage.
8. never criticize.
9. avoid touchy subjects.
10. say, "I always have time for you," and prove it!

Along with interest demonstrated on both sides, there must be a growing *delight* in knowing one another better, for that is the greatest incentive to intimacy. If you enjoy each other's company and the sharing of experiences, you are well on the way to an intimate marriage. In such a setting neither partner minds opening up to the other, because both have the confidence that if they are better known, they will be loved more.

As a husband told us, "Getting to know my wife during the first five years of our marriage has been a fascinating experience. We had gone through the University of Wyoming together, and we considered ourselves best friends when we were engaged. But I found I didn't really know her, after all. She's more beautiful than I imagined she could be . . . and I'm still learning."

4. Remember that sex is no substitute for intimacy.

This is something that women understand, but men sometimes do not. Women have both the need and desire to relate in other ways before they are ready for sex. They tend to be social before they are sexual; in contrast, men have been conditioned to be primarily sexual and to express their needs for intimacy through intercourse.

For instance, when a man comes home to his wife after a week away on business, she wants to hug him and kiss him and talk to him and feel close to him again. He wants to regain closeness by immediately having intercourse with her. She's hurt because "all he wants is my body." He's hurt because she has misunderstood his attempt to be intimate through sexual lovemaking, and he feels rejected.

Men may see no fine shade of difference between sex and intimacy, but their wives will, unless sex takes place after the exchange of mutual tenderness in an environment of emotional closeness. Impersonal sex intensifies loneliness; true sexual intimacy has great power to refresh the entire marriage.

5. *Fill your marriage with tender, nonsexual physical touching.*

Consider the dictionary definition of *caress:* An act of endearment, a tender or loving embrace. To touch, stroke, pat — tenderly, lovingly, or softly. This is what we are suggesting: touching as a communication of private intimacy, not as a sexual signal. Try hugs, holding hands, and all the gentle gestures which say so much. Even a smile or a wink across the room builds the enjoyment of intimacy. Eye contact provides the spark of understanding that you need. Hold hands when you pray; take time for closeness morning and night; sit so that you are touching in some way instead of choosing chairs across the room; leave each other and greet each other with a special kiss. This kind of touching becomes the tangible base of your intimate relationship.

We will have more to say about touching in the next chapter, for it is also an important part of nurturing.

6. *Maintain the we perspective.*

When we talk to couples who are having problems with intimacy, invariably their sentences begin with *I.*

Seldom, if ever, do they use *we*. People who are only interested in themselves just do not have the capacity to build an intimate relationship, even though they may crave the benefits of intimacy.

To maintain the *we* perspective, you will have to forget what today's culture claims about the importance of self-fulfillment. We've become a nation of individuals operating on the *I must always do what's best for me* principle. This can be disastrous to an intimate relationship, which requires both partners to be open and vulnerable to one another. As one wife said, "Don't talk to me about opening up to my husband. I can't trust myself to him. He only looks out for himself, and I'm on my own." Intimacy in marriage always depends upon the knowledge that each of you will look out for the other, and in that knowledge you can feel secure.

A word of warning: Newlyweds find it easy to use the word "we" at first. But listen to yourself in a year or two. If "I" begins cropping up more and more in the words you speak — as well as in your thoughts — it indicates that a sense of distance and loss of intimacy has already occurred, and you will need to take quick action to restore it.

7. *Communicate approval and acceptance of one another*.

Everyone fears disapproval, especially from the one we love most. This fear is probably the greatest hindrance to intimacy in an otherwise good marriage. As a husband explained, "It isn't that my wife rejects me. She's really very loving. But she's always pointing out to me — in a nice way, of course — what I did wrong or what I should have done instead. I get so tired of the feeling that she's disapproving of me. I know I don't quite measure up, and I can't enjoy being close to her anymore."

Granted, you will have differences of opinion and even strong clashes as you learn to resolve conflicts in your new life together. But you need to communicate an approval and acceptance of one another that runs far deeper than these surface matters. When you disagree on an issue, do it gently in a respectful way. Always discuss in the context of love for your partner, which is more important than the issue at hand.

Also remember that the major impact of communication comes from body language, facial expressions, and tone of voice. You may be communicating disapproval in those modes even though your words say something else. *Of all the things you wear, your expression is the most important.*

8. *Recognize and overcome fear of intimacy by building trust in actions, words, and attitudes.*

Although people need and even long for intimacy, they sometimes react to it with fear. Or withdraw if it becomes a possibility. Why? Because intimacy represents a mutual need for closeness, and people are often afraid to *need* someone else. In the past they may have been let down and disappointed by those they depended on (sometimes parents), and they do not want to risk it again. Or they are afraid of revealing their true self to their lover (a necessity in an intimate relationship), afraid that if the lover knew what was "behind the mask" they would be abandoned.

Other related fears include fear of criticism, fear of

rejection, and fear of being used. All these fears can be put under one umbrella labeled: *I am afraid of being hurt.*

Without trust, no real emotional intimacy is possible. To build this trust in your relationship, follow these basic principles:

a. Always be very kind to one another.
b. Never reject the other, or shut the door to touching, talking, or sharing your life with your mate.
c. Build trust through *faithfulness.* (See chapter three of our new-marriage handbook, *The First Years of Forever.*)

Here are key characteristics of the kind of intimate relationship which will overcome all future fears:

A committed relationship

You know that when you go to your loved one, he or she will always take you in. This is part of the *at homeness* present in an intimate marriage. (Think of Robert Frost's description of home: Home is the place where when you go there, they have to take you in.)

A relationship without exploitation

You demonstrate to one another by deed as well as word: "I don't want to use you. I want to love you."

An open relationship

No hiding is necessary because you know you are accepted unconditionally. You can trust each other enough to become vulnerable, knowing you will not be under attack, but accepted and loved just as you are.

A mutual support system

You can go to your lover whenever you feel low or lonely or misunderstood. As someone has said, "When you respond to me so that I feel special, it will make up for all those who, during the day, have passed me by without seeing me." You are free to let one another know your emotional needs, and you do it because it is unfair to expect your partner to read your mind.

A treasured relationship

You appreciate this as one of the two most valuable treasures of life, the other being a personal relationship with God. You know you possess this intimate closeness by mutual choice and deep desire, and you both do everything possible to preserve it forever.

9. *Maintain the spirit of discovery in your relationship.*

When you married, each of you left your old world to form a new one together. You have entered into a new reality where two are in the process of becoming one. And the new world you longed for when you fell in love is now yours for the taking. It's up to you to explore the territory, take dominion over it, and make it what you both want it to be. Think of yourselves as pioneers who, because you are entering new territory, must explore it and establish your lives in the new world.

You will need to establish an atmosphere of permanence and safety in which both partners can experience intimacy, a new world in which you can safely express love and grow in love together. You will need your own language of love for this new reality. It's important to gain an awareness of what makes your partner *feel* loved. Both of you should share this information, being as specific as possible. Think back to a time in your past when you felt totally loved. Remember how it felt. Reexperience those feelings and try to find the key ingredient. Then you can tell your partner, (for instance) "The thing that makes me feel most loved is . . . when you touch me gently on the face, and look at me searchingly."

To know specifically what makes your partner feel loved is a major discovery, and one which many spouses never make. It's strange how many people try to love their mate the way they themselves want to be loved, disregarding the fact that their partner has a different language.

Building up this special vocabulary, this collection of private things you say and do which have great meaning for both of you, is part of establishing your new world of intimacy, your new reality. It will include secret names for each other, inside jokes, actions which privately express great tenderness or indicate physical desire, shared memories, and words which send special signals to each other.

Many couples enjoy some of this during courtship but forget it when they settle into their marriage. You not only have to *pioneer* your new world, you have to stay alert and involved to *preserve* your new world.

Here's another reason why you must *maintain* the spirit of discovery. All through life you will be changing — both of you — in your own ways according to the process which has been called "adult unfolding." You must expect this and understand that your marriage is a living, and thus changing relationship. Fundamental, unchanging truths undergird a marriage, but these principles are lived out by human beings who change and grow and encounter problems of one kind or another all along the way. To become one, and to remain one through all the changes and vicissitudes of life is a great challenge.

The surest way of remaining in a state of oneness is to grow in spiritual intimacy, establishing the lifelong habit of Bible reading and prayer together in a special private time which is enjoyed daily. If you continue to move in the same direction spiritually, allowing your lives to be shaped and readjusted by biblical principles and the work of the Holy Spirit, you will be able to be flexible in your dealings with one another, and able to change together, instead of separately.

Is your new world a perfect one? Certainly not. If the time of falling in love is a Garden experience, we leave Eden when we marry, and we learn to live in a new environment (at times, a gray world) according to our vision of love. That's why it's so important to share the same vision, and to have it continually reshaped, refreshed, and even refocused by the truth of God's Word — God who is the source of all love.

10. *Follow the pattern of Ephesians 4:22 – 24 in making your choices for intimacy.*

Begin by considering what will happen if you ignore the need to create an emotional climate of intimacy in your relationship. The alternative is emotional distance, with its inevitable components of disinterest, or distrust, or even dislike and open hostility. The prefix *dis* generally denotes *separation, negation,* or *reversal.* If the two of you want to build a love-filled, lasting marriage, it's safe to assume that you don't want separation from one another, or negatives in your relationship, or reversals of all you have hoped for.

The choice belongs to you. You will have countless opportunities to make choices that draw you together into a wonderful intimacy, and you'll have just as many temptations to make selfish, foolish choices that would certainly pull you apart and set distance between you. This, then, is a good time to revisit Ephesians 4:22 – 24; it will show you how to defuse the temptations and take advantage of the opportunities.

(1) PUT OFF AND DISCARD YOUR OLD UNRENEWED SELF WHICH IS BEING CORRUPTED BY ITS DECEITFUL DESIRES. Note that self-centered desires deceive us and trick us into making mistakes which will harm us. When selfishness runs unchecked in a marriage, it invariably corrupts. The Greek word for *corrupt* has three graphic meanings: shrivel, wither, and spoil. If self-centered desires take control, our love relationship may shrivel up and wither away. But God gives us the ability to discard the behavior which could lead to disaster. As Phillips's translation says, "Fling off the dirty clothes of the old way of living."

(2) BE CONSTANTLY RENEWED IN THE SPIRIT OF YOUR MIND, HAVING A FRESH MENTAL AND SPIRITUAL ATTITUDE. Let God keep your mind refreshed with truth and positive counsel from the Scriptures

which can help you think clearly and rightly about the choices of your marriage.

(3) PUT ON THE NEW NATURE CREATED IN GOD'S IMAGE IN TRUE RIGHTEOUSNESS AND HOLINESS. As Phillips translates it, "Put on the clean fresh clothes of the new life which was made by God's design." This is the behavior that will bless you and bless your marriage. God says, Put it on. Choose to do it, and God will give you the power to accomplish it.

Intimacy can be yours if you desire it and choose to pursue it. Pursue it patiently, consistently, and delicately, with sensitivity. Nothing is more vulnerable to fluctuations, changes, and influences — positive or negative — than your intimate relationship. It is fueled by shared feelings, and the slightest turning away will be felt by the intimate lover-friend. If the chill of misunderstanding or the heat of annoyance threatens your closeness, forgive freely and be quick to reconcile. Test your choices by these questions: Will this produce a positive response or a negative response? Will it build our relationship or tear it down? As a result of this, will we be closer emotionally or farther apart?

Protect your intimacy as the treasure of your marriage, and enjoy!

Make a once-for-all decision to take the path to intimacy, and test all you do and say by the question, "Will this draw us closer or move us apart?" This is the eighth step in building a great marriage.

SUGGESTIONS

1. Take this "Test for Intimacy," inserting your answers in your notebook. Plan to take it weekly as a means of checking the emotional temperature of your relationship and charting changes. Any no answer should alert you to a possible problem, or to an area which you need to develop. Remember the principle of "delicate pursuit."

Test for Intimacy

(1) Do you and your partner talk about feelings?

(2) Do you usually understand what your partner is feeling? Does your partner understand you?

(3) Do each of you trust the other and feel safe from hurt?

(4) Do you touch lovingly and often?

(5) Do you and your partner usually share a good feeling of closeness that seems to make everything else "worthwhile?"

(6) Have you moved closer this week or drawn apart?

2. Study chapters 3 and 5 on "Faithfulness" and "Communication" in our new-marriage handbook, *The First Years of Forever*. Make notes from these chapters on how to build trust in your marriage and how to communicate your feelings. Record them in the intimacy section of your notebook.

3. Become an expert on the one book of the Bible devoted exclusively to love and marriage. In the Song of Songs, God presents a vivid picture of an intimate marriage which you can use as a model for your own relationship. Read and reread this book in a modern

translation, recording ideas and ways to apply what you learn in your notebook.

4. Apply Ephesians 4:22 – 24 to the phase of your relationship which seems to need attention. These questions can guide you in determining what you want and need to do in God's power.

> (1) What do you need, want, and choose to put aside?
> (2) What attitudes need to be changed within you?
> (3) What new behavior do you need, want, and choose to put on as your own?

5

NEGLECT OR NURTURING

Are we taking good care of one another or ignoring the other's needs?

"This is now bone of my bones, and flesh of my flesh" (Gen. 2:23 NASB).

For no one ever hated his own flesh, but nourishes and cherishes it (Eph. 5:29 NASB).

In this chapter we leave the delights of intimacy and turn to the area of marital interaction called *nurturing*, which is nothing less than our responsibility to take care of one another and meet each other's needs for a lifetime.

If this sounds like a very large order, it is. Perhaps that's why people seldom write about nurturing: it requires so much from us. Intimacy is an enjoyable sharing of ourselves with one another; nurturing is giving to our partner, even though it costs us. Intimacy requires that we become *we*-centered; nurturing demands that we become *other*-centered — and that's not easy for people who are inherently *self*-centered. Nowhere in marriage does the separation between selfishness and unselfishness show up more distinctly. Nowhere is the opportunity greater to build oneness by meeting the other's needs; by giving. But equally great is the temptation to build a wall of alienation by ignoring the other's needs; by taking all we can get.

As we consider our secret choices in this area of marriage, we need to recognize that on our own we will find it very difficult to make the right choices consistently. And if we fail in this matter, or fail to try, our marriage will bear the scars.

What we cannot do on our own, God will give us the resources to accomplish. We will have good reason to hope if we keep our sights on God's plan for our relationship — His principle of nurturing in marriage; His pattern of love strengthened by loyalty; and His power to enable us to keep our marriage vows with the stubborn, steadfast loving-kindness the Bible calls *hesed.*

THE ARRANGEMENT: WHO TAKES CARE OF WHOM AND HOW

In every marriage an arrangement evolves which determines "who takes care of whom and how." If both partners are satisfied with the arrangement, their marriage is blessed with harmony and positive reactions to the reassurance and comfort of being loved. When both partners are nurtured in the ways they desire, they feel loved, and when two people *feel* loved, they feel like *loving.* A husband and wife in this frame of mind can give freely to one another, and keep on giving with generosity of heart.

By contrast, where husband and wife fail to care for each other's physical and emotional needs, a cycle of neglect, complaints, resentments, and angry demands gains momentum. Eventually, if no change for the better occurs, chronic disagreements turn into ongoing battles, while lovers turn into enemies, or look elsewhere for the care and attention they desire.

In other words, the stakes are high. Nurturing matters very much in the delicate balance of your relationship. Newlyweds seldom give this a thought when they marry, but it can become an area of conflict rather quickly thereafter.

The fact is that we never outgrow our need for nurturing. It reaches back to our earliest experiences, before language dawned for us, when we learned to trust the person taking care of us. The beneath-the-surface memories of that time have become a part of us and have shaped our needs and expectations today. We still tend to measure how much we are loved by how well our physical and emotional needs are met. And each of us has a unique agenda of needs, charged with meanings, which we expect our marriage partner to give attention to.

For example, one husband expects his wife to remember which foods he likes and dislikes, and gets moody if she serves something on the forbidden list; another wants his clothes kept in top condition and available on demand. One wife needs a luxury gift every few months; another has a strong need for continued verbal assurances of her husband's love. For some people sexual needs take front ranking; for others it's a craving for intimate talks. One wife gets nervous in grocery stores and depends on her husband to do all the marketing; a husband feels inadequate on the telephone and counts on his wife to take care of all the household business calls. Another husband demands pampering in bed when he has the mildest cold, and when his wife has to go to the doctor, she insists on being taken, rather than driving herself. Granted, these may sound (to someone else) like luxuries rather than needs, but that is not the issue. If something represents a serious need to one partner, the other mate, if wise and loving, will be sensitive to it, and will demonstrate a caring, compassionate response.

It's of burning importance to us to feel that our partner cares enough to meet our special needs. If our needs are unmet or, even worse, completely ignored, we may not discuss them directly, but we will express our discontent, anger, and frustration in other ways. The negative words and actions which invade the marriage should be understood for what they are: expressions of protest.

The principle to remember is that everyone desires and needs some kind of nurturing. It's up to each of us to learn what our partner regards as his or her most important needs, and to determine whether we are meeting them or neglecting them. We also should take time to think about other needs our partner has, but will not admit, and how we can help meet those needs. One of the prime secrets of a happy home is finding out what matters to our partner and then *doing it.* When both partners follow this prescription and take care of one another *in ways that count,* the resulting harmony is close to "heaven on earth."

> Create an emotional climate of caring by find-
> ing out what nurtures your partner and then
> doing it, gladly and lovingly. This is the ninth
> step in building a successful marriage.

As time passes and changes occur, new responsibilities may hinder us from giving our accustomed care
and attention to one another. This will place an undeni-
able strain on our relationship. Even desirable changes,
as well as those we'd rather avoid, can produce tensions. Pregnancy, illness, a relative moving into our
home, a demanding new job which takes all our attention for awhile, a return to college for advanced education, and the care of aging or ill parents head the list of
factors which affect the quality and quantity of nurturing we can give one another. This, in turn, may create
strong dissatisfaction with the marriage. Whenever circumstances change, we need to make the necessary
adjustments in our relationship with special tact and
demonstrations of our continuing love for one another.

No matter what we do to nurture one another, the
way we do it is of supreme importance. In fact, if we do
it the wrong way, it's not nurturing at all. The value of a
willing, glad-to-be-helpful spirit and a gracious attitude
in caring for one another generously and without complaint is beyond measure.

Finally, we should remember as we make daily
choices that in this area of interaction, little things
mean a lot!

*   *   *

NURTURING IN MARRIAGE: A BIBLICAL PRINCIPLE

Is it possible to go on nurturing our partner when our own needs are being ignored? How about the times when we feel too much is being asked of us, and we're tempted to say, "Take care of yourself. Do it yourself. I'm not your mother (or father)!"

Those words sound a bit like Cain's, don't they? (The selfish displeasure, the fallen countenance, "Am I my brother's keeper?") It's true, we're not a parent (or a sibling); we're much closer than that. We are *one flesh*, and the Bible makes it as clear as sunlight that we *are* responsible for our mate. Pride, self-centeredness, and self-pity will tempt us to react with foolish choices that can harm us and destroy our marriage. In contrast, God's plan is simple and beneficial: we are to give our partner the loving attention we give to our own body. Our ability to make good choices in our marriage, even when we are tempted to do the opposite, depends upon how precise our knowledge is of God's plan for marriage, and how willing we are to trust His wisdom and apply it in our lives.

Here is the biblical principle of nurturing in marriage from Ephesians 5:28 – 29 in several different translations.

> So ought men to love their wives as their own bodies. He that loveth his wife loveth himself. For no man ever yet hated his own flesh; but nourisheth and cherisheth it, even as the Lord the church (KJV).

> In this same way, husbands ought to love their wives as their own bodies. He who loves his wife

loves himself. After all, no one ever hated his own body, but he feeds and cares for it, just as Christ does the church (NIV).

Men ought to give their wives the love they naturally have for their own bodies. The love a man gives his wife is the extending of his love for himself to enfold her. (Phillips).

We can learn a lot about how to nurture our partner by understanding the two key words in this passage: *nourishing* (feeding and aiding in the other's development by providing what is needed) and *cherishing* (caring for). Let's take a closer look at *cherishing*, for it offers three important guidelines. First, cherishing involves taking care of tenderly, keeping our loved one warm the way birds cover their young with feathers, and protecting our mate as a hen shields her chicks from harm. Second, cherishing involves display of affection. Cherish comes from the same root word as *caress* and speaks of providing the physical affection our partner needs. Finally, to cherish means to encourage or support. The emotional support and reassurance partners give, and the practical ways they help each other through life are all part of the nurturing process.

The amount of nurturing we provide should be compatible with the love we have for our own self: we are to love and care for our mate as much as we love and care for our own flesh. But note that the commandment to love in this way is directed to the husband; he nurtures, and his wife responds. She has her own responsibilities in the relationship, and they are given to her (1) at the beginning of this passage where she is

instructed to willingly adapt herself to her husband —
by implication, preparing herself to meet his needs; and
(2) at its conclusion where she is directed to hold her
husband in a position of respect.

> You wives must learn to adapt yourselves to your
> husbands, as you submit yourselves to the
> Lord. . . . In practice what I have said amounts to
> this: let every one of you who is a husband love
> his wife as he loves himself, and let the wife rever-
> ence her husband (Eph. 5:22, 33 Phillips).

Why did the Lord arrange it this way? Some have
suggested that the Lord knew husbands would have to
be commanded to love and nurture their wives, while
wives, designed for potential motherhood, would possess the natural ability and the inclination to nurture
those they loved. Others have countered that the Lord
also knew wives would have to be commanded to
demonstrate respect for their husbands and to submit
graciously to their leadership. For both husbands and
wives, some sacrifice of natural tendencies is involved.

One thing we can be sure of: The Lord has shown
us what each partner needs *most*. Women need love;
men need respect. Women especially need nourishing
and cherishing for their well-being; men especially
need a positive response to their leadership to encourage them to carry out the position of responsibility
which God has given them. Consider Ephesians 5:33
again, this time in the Amplified translation:

> However, let each man of you (without exception)
> love his wife as (being in a sense) his very own self;

and let the wife see that she respects and reverences her husband — that she notices him, regards him, honors him, prefers him, venerates and esteems him; and that she defers to him, praises him, and loves and admires him exceedingly.

In a good marriage both partners will find pleasure in nurturing their mates physically, emotionally, and spiritually, giving each other all they need to mature and reach their God-designed potential. Because, as we pointed out earlier, this is such a large order, it's well to have a plan to follow in making the right choices consistently. We have one to suggest — a tried and proven prescription for your marriage.

THE B-E-S-T PLAN FOR NURTURING

We originally developed this plan to help couples rekindle their love for one another. Think of it as a formula to remind you of your partner's needs and the biblical way to meet them. The plan is practical — it gives you things to do; uncomplicated — you can remember it easily; and effective — it really works for any couple motivated enough to apply it in their marriage. It doesn't even require both partners to make it work. If only *one* person wants a transformed marriage, this plan for nurturing can be put into motion with positive results. When two live it out, the rewards keep on multiplying.

The B-E-S-T plan is based on three facts:
(1) Love is the power that produces love.

    (2) Giving is love in action; giving is love made visible.

    (3) You can lovingly nurture your partner and spark an answering love by giving the B-E-S-T:

- •BLESSING
- •EDIFYING
- •SHARING
- •TOUCHING

As we describe the four parts of this plan and give you some suggestions in applying each part, remember that they need to be set into motion simultaneously, not one at a time. When you are blessing, it becomes easier to touch; when you are edifying, it becomes more enjoyable to share. The four patterns of behavior reinforce one another and quadruple the benefits.

Consistency is important too. The B-E-S-T treatment needs to become a habit, not a happy surprise with which to dazzle your partner now and then. Trust comes from steady, unchanging behavior, and one mistake can tear down what you have spent many weeks building.

BLESSING

Blessing is a New Testament word *eulogia,* taken from two Greek words, *eu* which means "well" and *logos* which means "word." This will remind you of the first way to bless your partner: Speak well of him or her and always answer with good words even though you feel you have just been scolded, scorned, ignored, or insulted.

The Lord Jesus, who did not answer in turn when He was reviled, is our pattern of behavior. *In the same way,* the Scripture says, we are to live as husbands and wives. We have no justification for speaking to our partner scornfully, angrily, or manipulatively. Even when our partner behaves badly, we do not have license to retaliate. If we fail to bless, God says that we will miss out on the blessing which He has called us to receive.

Think about it. If you bless your partner by the words you speak, and the times when you choose to hold your peace, you will avoid the damage inflicted on new marriages by two angry people with uncontrolled tongues. Afterward, when they want to reconcile, there's a lot to forgive and forget. An angry spirit and a raging tongue can never nourish and cherish. The Bible reminds us,

> A SOFT answer turneth away wrath, but grievous words stir up anger (Prov. 15:1 KJV).

> To sum up, let all be harmonious, sympathetic, brotherly, kind-hearted, and humble in spirit; not returning evil for evil, or insult for insult, but giving a blessing instead; for you were called for the very purpose that you might inherit a blessing. For "let him who means to love life and see good days refrain his tongue from evil and his lips from speaking guile. And let him turn away from evil and do good; let him seek peace and pursue it. For the eyes of the Lord are upon the righteous, and His ears attend to their prayer but the face of the Lord is against those who do evil" (1 Peter 3:8 – 12 NASB).

The second way to bless your partner is by doing

kind things for him or her — not as a duty but as a gift of blessing. Think about what your partner really likes. His socks put together in a certain way (which seems like a waste of time to you)? Her pleasure in a freshly made cup of coffee before she gets out of bed? It can be something small, but perfectly suited to your partner's private tastes and wishes. You fill in the blanks. You know best how to bless your partner with *kindness in action*.

The third way to bless is by showing thankfulness and appreciation. Whatever you appreciate in your partner, make it known verbally. Thank your partner with the same courtesy you would show to an outsider — plus a lot more warmth!

The fourth way to bless is by calling God's favor down in prayer for your partner's highest good and best welfare. Some people spend time praying for missions and ministries but forget that no one needs or deserves their prayers more than their own marriage partner.

To review, you nurture your partner and enhance your marriage by blessing with (1) good words; (2) kind actions; (3) thankful appreciation; and (4) intercessory prayer. Blessing not only prevents the spread of mutual hostility but opens the door to God's blessing upon both of you and your marriage.

TWELVE WAYS TO NURTURE YOUR PARTNER BY BLESSING

The Key to Love

1. Say something good about your partner to another person.

2. Answer with positive, loving words, no matter what.
3. Do something kind for your mate.
4. Surprise him or her with a gift or thoughtful act.
5. Do the things you know are important to your loved one.
6. Say "thank you" often and mean it. Say "I love you."
7. Be consistently courteous.
8. Thank God for your mate. Be specific.
9. Pray for his or her blessing.
10. Choose to forgive if hurt or offended.
11. Avoid proud behavior and never try to get even.
12. Study more ways to bless your partner.

EDIFYING

D. James Kennedy, in his helpful book, *Learning to Live with the People You Love,* points out that marriage can be either tremendously constructive or unimaginably destructive to the lives of those involved. What makes the difference? In essence, **building up** or **tearing down** one's partner.

He reminds us how, when we fell in love, we knew we had met the most wonderful person in the world, and we had no patience with family or friends who tried to point out a flaw in our loved one. Our way of seeing one another had positive results, because we began to become the person our beloved thought that we could be.

But what if, instead of continuing this constructive and encouraging pattern, we discovered that our mate did indeed have faults? If we concentrated on the negatives, our view of the good points would become blurred, and all that made us discontented with our partner would move into sharp focus.

If we began to communicate our changed viewpoint and our new opinion to our partner, our partner would slowly become what we believed him or her to be. *What you say is usually what you get!*

To prevent this destructive cycle of behavior, learn to nurture each other with the gift of *edifying*. This biblical term, often used in the New Testament, refers to the building up of individuals. When you edify your partner, you build her up in every aspect of her personality. You cheer him on in every area of life and increase his sense of self-worth so that his capacity to love and give will be increased too. To edify is to personally encourage. Because edifying builds up and never tears down, you give your partner freedom to grow and develop as a person without fear of failure or hurtful criticism.

Edifying begins in the life of the mind, where Philippians 4:8 is applied: "If there is any excellence and if anything worthy of praise, let your mind dwell on these things" (NASB). Practice thinking about things you find attractive in your mate — every positive quality your partner possesses. Ask yourself this before you speak: Will these words build up or tear down? And ask yourself: What can I say to my partner right now that will edify and build up, encourage, strengthen, and bring peace?

Did you know that praise is actually a source of fresh

energy which can be measured in the laboratory? Dr. Henry H. Goddard pioneered these studies, using an instrument devised to measure fatigue. When an assistant would say to the tired child at the instrument, "You're doing fine, John," the boy's energy-curve would actually soar. Discouragement and fault-finding were found to have an opposite effect which could also be measured! Imagine the miracles you could achieve by nurturing your partner with genuine appreciation and encouragement.

When you nurture, you provide a place of emotional safety. The husband and wife who are afraid of hurt, rebuff, criticism, and misunderstanding from the other will find it difficult to touch and share freely. So it's important to learn how to establish trust. Let this be your guide:

(1) Love covers over a multitude of sins (1 Peter 4:8).
(2) Love builds up (1 Cor. 8:1).

Edifying not only offers a place of safety, but will quickly spark an interested response in a partner who has been showing indifference. All people love to be edified and will be drawn to the one who builds them up.

TWELVE WAYS TO NURTURE YOUR PARTNER BY EDIFYING

The Key to Well-Being

1. Decide not to criticize your partner again. Back up your decision by action until it becomes a habit.
2. Discern where your partner can use extra

encouragement and think of ways to build him or her up.

3. Spend some time thinking about every positive quality you admire in your mate.

4. Edify your partner with words of praise and appreciation. Be genuine, specific, generous.

5. Recognize his or her talents, abilities, and accomplishments.

6. Communicate your respect for the work he or she does.

7. Keep your attention focused on your partner rather than expressing admiration for others of the opposite sex.

8. Seek your partner's opinions and show that you value his or her judgment.

9. Demonstrate your confidence in him or her.

10. Respond to your mate with eye contact, smiles, and body language (turning toward him or her).

11. Treat your partner as a VIP in your home and in the presence of others.

12. Provide a peaceful, relaxed atmosphere of acceptance and unconditional love.

SHARING

The more ways you can find to be in relationship with each other, the less lonely you are, and the stronger your love will become. People are drawn into loving closeness because of what they share. In fact, *sharing* has been called the central secret of enduring love.

Sharing should touch all areas of life — your time,

activities, pleasures, interests and concerns, ideas and innermost thoughts, family objectives and goals, and, most important, your spiritual values and the way you express them.

This might be a good time for you to think creatively about how to give one another the gift of sharing. Consider your life in these five areas, incorporating your ideas and conclusions into your Master Plan:

- Common Ground. Think of the things you share right now. How can you enjoy it more?
- Separate Ground. Areas of work and responsibility may be separate, but how can you bridge the gaps to share your different worlds?
- New Ground for One. What interests can you learn to enjoy because your partner enjoys them? How can you develop new enthusiasms to match your partner's?
- New Ground for Both. Can you think of some absorbing new interests to develop together?
- Higher Ground. Are you sharing your spiritual life through prayer, Bible reading, church participation, and special ministries? Is it satisfying to both?

At no time is your sharing more meaningful than when the values supremely important to you are held in common, supported, and expressed together. The most beautiful song of marriage is not a duet (pleasant though that is), but a three-part harmony which husband, wife, and the Lord God produce as a sweet agreement — an inner togetherness. And when you have a common faith, *prayer together* is the key to sharing the joy of it.

Billy Graham, married for more than forty years, believes also that a successful marriage is made up of three people: husband, wife, and God, and he says that he and his wife have never faced a problem which could not be solved with love, forgiveness, and prayer.

Unfortunately, it's estimated that only about one percent of husbands and wives in America have meaningful prayer together. This has been called a tragic statistic, because prayer can cement a marriage together. Many couples find that the problems in their relationship — anger, pride, hurt, misunderstandings, or resentments — seem to melt away in the presence of a holy and loving God as they pray together.

One husband told us, "When we pray for each other, about eighty percent of it is thanksgiving. It energizes us and keeps us in harmony, and open to one another, when otherwise we might choose to keep our distance (and hurt our relationship in the process). I wonder how married couples manage without a prayer life together!"

When couples spend a lifetime nurturing one another through sharing, the result is the *oneness* God designed to alleviate man and woman's loneliness. A husband described it this way, "It is difficult to know where 'she' begins and 'I' leave off."

TWELVE WAYS TO NURTURE YOUR PARTNER BY SHARING

The Key to Oneness

1. Enjoy some quality time together every day.

2. Do a special project together.
3. Develop some new interest in common.
4. Learn more about one another's work. Share the challenges and the rewards.
5. Enjoy a special date together once a week. Plan for it.
6. Listen to him or her attentively without interrupting.
7. Be understanding. Share your feelings. Say "I care, I love you."
8. Make plans, set goals together.
9. Do housework or yard work together and make it fun.
10. Study communication skills together and practice them.
11. Treat your partner the way you would treat your best friend. (Your partner *should* be your best friend.)
12. Pray together, grow in faith, share a ministry together.

TOUCHING

The fourth element in the B-E-S-T plan for nurturing is the easiest to implement and, in some ways, the most important. Touching, of course, represents the physical care and attention we must give to one another, but it means much more than that. Touching kindles a flame which every marriage needs. In fact, physical contact, apart from sex, is absolutely essential in keeping the fires of romantic love lit between husband and wife. The people who come into Dr. Wheat's office saying, "I love my partner but I'm just not *in love* with him (or her)" are the ones who have very little affectionate touching in their marriage — no hugs or love pats or holding hands, no kisses "just because," and no snuggling close to each other at night.

It's ironic that young couples who have built an intense love relationship by holding hands, kissing, hugging, and cuddling while they were dating often quit touching after marriage. Why give it up when it's so enjoyable? Because touch has become only a sexual signal in their relationship, and something irreplaceable has been lost.

Touching is important to us all of the time! Scientists believe that the inescapable need for skin contact is more crucial than hunger for food. Researchers have found that human infants and baby monkeys have trouble surviving without skin touch in their early months. Touch deprivation causes withdrawal, failure to thrive, infant depression, and even death.

Adults can also suffer from touch deprivation, and *touch hunger* is a common marital problem. Your partner's need, as well as your own need to be held nonsexually for comfort and to be touched tenderly and gently in nurturing ways, should be recognized and met in the security of marriage.

Anyone can learn to touch by doing it. People may claim that they don't enjoy it (usually because their family never learned to touch), but we have found in our work with couples that when people actually try it, they like it! People who had never learned to say freely, "I love you," find that they can do so and want to do so after a little experience with touching and being touched in loving, nonsexual ways. Authorities on touch say that one of the measures of our development as healthy human beings is the extent to which we are freely able to embrace and enjoy the nonsexual embraces of others.

In marriage touching is the least threatening way to bridge the distance created by other problems. In times of strong emotion, people respond best to physical contact rather than talking. Remember how a hug from Mom made everything feel better, how a little child goes to Mom or Dad to get the hurt kissed away? We need to go back to the beautiful simplicity of this in our marriage. Couples who have learned how to give and receive affectionate touching — a pat on the shoulder, a squeeze of the hand, a caress of the cheek, a strength-imparting hug, physical closeness, whether watching TV or listening to a sermon — say that this brings them feelings of comfort, optimism, support, and togetherness that are truly wonderful.

Stop and appreciate the way God designed touch as a blessing for your marriage. It is the most personally experienced of all sensations available to human beings. Our skin has been created to register this good experience. Experts say that the skin's sensitivity is so great and its ability to transmit signals so extraordinary, that for versatility it must be ranked second only to the brain.

So, explore the pleasures of touch, apart from sex. Learn to give each other gentle, nurturing massages, using a pleasing lotion or scented oil. This produces relaxation, a lowered heart rate, lowered blood pressure, and lets you experience the thrills of being in love. That's a lot of benefit for an hour's enjoyable activity. Have times of pleasure-oriented caressing without sex as your goal. Avoid the genital area and discover other sensitive areas of your body. Learn to please and to anticipate one another's desires. Teach one another what you like best by responding positively to the touch sensations you enjoy. Most people learn the language of loving through touch rather quickly, once they focus their attention on it.

Then become sensitive to the ways you can keep in touch in daily life. (Dr. Wheat prefers love seats in his house!) Hold hands when you walk, never separate without a good-bye kiss, and find times to hug when there is no reason except the good feeling it gives to both of you.

Use our list of suggestions as a take-off point to spark the individual creativity you can put into your own marriage through the avenue of touching.

TWELVE WAYS TO NURTURE YOUR PARTNER BY TOUCHING

The Key to Romance

1. Hug often for no particular reason.
2. Always greet or leave with a kiss. Kiss when there's no occasion.
3. Sit close to each other, whether in church or at home watching TV.
4. Go to bed at the same time and cuddle before you go to sleep. Allow a few minutes in the morning to hold each other before you get up.
5. Show as much concern for your partner's body as you do for your own.

6. Practice expressing your love through the medium of tender touch. Find out what feels good to your partner.

7. Give each other back rubs, massages. Use a pleasing lotion or scented oil. Enjoy!

8. Take your shower or bath together. Be lighthearted and sensuous.

9. Develop positive feelings toward your own body (See Ps. 139:13, 14).

10. Stay in physical contact while going to sleep.

11. Hold hands when you take a walk. Enjoy the thrill of holding hands anytime.

12. Think of ways to say *I love you* by tender touch.

If you want to know how the B-E-S-T plan can transform a marriage, read the book *Rekindled* (Revell, 1985), which tells how a husband set out to nurture his wife and restore intimacy to their marriage by applying the B-E-S-T principles as he found them in our book, *LOVE LIFE for Every Married Couple*. *Rekindled* describes, in vivid detail, what happens when even one partner cares enough to put this plan into practice. But please remember that the B-E-S-T plan is not just an emergency measure for crisis situations. It's one of the best things you can do for your marriage right now.

> Put the B-E-S-T plan for nurturing your partner into effect and follow it consistently. This is the tenth step in creating a marriage filled with all good pleasures.

WHEN NURTURING BECOMES A NECESSITY

Nurturing one another in marriage can be pleasant and delightful, but at some point it may become a hard necessity. As adults, we prefer to think we will always be capable of looking after ourselves. Yet we realize the time might come when we will need help. After a serious accident or an emotional collapse, during the course of a terminal illness, or if other infirmities of mind or body should overtake us, will our marriage partner be there to do for us what we cannot do for ourselves?

Almost all wedding vows include promises to cherish one another in the worst as well as the best conditions. Did your vows follow this pattern? *In hardships and in triumphs . . . in want and in plenty . . . in sorrow and in joy . . . in sickness and in health . . . forsaking all others . . . for as long as we both shall live.*

One of the comforts of a good marriage is experiencing the peace of knowing that, no matter what happens, we can count on our mate. So it's vital, from the day we marry, that we build our sense of confidence in one another.

The Scriptures say that "Confidence in an unfaithful (person) in time of trouble is like a broken tooth or a foot out of joint" (Prov. 25:19 AMPLIFIED). Two sad examples of this in marriage come to mind. We recall a young wife named Sarah, who was left stranded in a state-operated facility in a northern city without family, friends, or financial help. Sarah was paralyzed in an automobile accident caused by her husband, who deserted her when the extent of her injuries was known. We also remember a wife of retirement age in a western state whose husband suffered a stroke which took away his ability to speak. His illness so upset her that she visited him only once in the nursing home and eventually moved to another state to be with relatives, leaving him behind.

In contrast to these stories, we have seen many more faithful wives and husbands caring for their mates in the hospital and at home with great devotion, and, if a nursing home was required, spending a part of every day there with them.

The answer to whether we will be able to count on one another in the future lies in how well and how graciously we are caring for one another now on a daily basis. We store up trust for the darkest times of life by the way we live in the light, and by the way we handle the minor crises. A warm hug, a reassuring word, a helping hand, a willingness to do whatever is needed without complaint — these prove what kind of marriage partners we are. For a successful marriage, we need the assurance that as long as both of us live, we will *be there,* looking after one another to the best of our ability.

It's been said that the simplest definition of trust is the feeling that another person is *for you.* Add the element of loyalty — the person is *for you* and *won't change* — and you have the trust that is essential for a happy marriage.

Do you want to be this kind of husband or wife — loyal, steadfast, unchanging in your love and your commitment to do the best for your partner? We have talked to people who said, in effect, "But I can't be like this. I really want to be, but I'm weak, I'm changeable, and I can't be expected to handle problems. When it's too much for me, I'll have to walk away."

This too is a choice, and the people who say, "I *can't*" have just made one. When you say, "I *will*, and I *can* because God will show me how," you are choosing to stay in the mainstream of God's plan for you, and He will provide exactly what you need.

Both the pattern for this steadfast, loyal love, and the power to live it, come from God, who nurtures His people with the faithful loving-kindness the Bible calls *hesed*. To help you make the best choices in your marriage, you need to acquaint yourself with this word and the special quality of love it describes.

STUBBORN, STEADFAST *HESED* LOVE

It's amazing that in one beautiful, comprehensive word, God has fully described the attitude which partners in a marriage covenant can and should demonstrate toward one another. Found in the Old Testament 245 times, *hesed* (sometimes spelled *hesedh* or *chesed*) possesses such extraordinary richness and depth of meaning that no equivalent word in the English language exists. Bible translators have used a wide range of words to try to convey its multifaceted message. Often the word love appears with a variety of adjectives: steadfast love, true love, unfailing love, constant love, strong love, wonderful love, and the like. Other families of words are used to denote mercy, goodness, favor, promise, devotion, kindness, and loyalty. Certainly it is one of the most important of God's words for love, and it offers sure guidance for our marriage. By consulting the studies of *hesed* by biblical scholars, we can draw out these facts to apply in our own relationship.

1. *Hesed* always indicates some kind of relationship; it is used to express the feeling between people who are in a close relationship, such as couples in a marriage covenant. This is a concept we can take for our own as husband and wife.

2. The central meaning of *hesed* is love expressed in two significant ways: first, through kindness; and second, through loyalty. These two qualities can be considered as the main building blocks in a stable, love-filled relationship.

3. The kindness of *hesed* blesses the relationship with a continuing attitude of goodwill which proves itself in action — good, kind actions which demonstrate favor out of deep affection for the beloved. Our marriage should be characterized by kindness — seen, experienced, and felt. Here is a scriptural example of *hesed* which we could take as a model for our own love relationship:

> The Lord appeared of old to me (Israel), saying,
> Yes, I have loved you with an everlasting love;
> therefore with loving-kindness have I drawn you
> and have continued My faithfulness to you (Jer.
> 31:3 AMPLIFIED).

4. The unshakable loyalty of *hesed* is dictated by duty as well as desire, so that if feelings fluctuate, our loyalty does not. This loyalty is directed in two ways: (1) to the persons involved and (2) to the promises made in the relationship. Here is a scriptural example of *hesed* which we could adopt as the love song of our marriage:

> "Though the mountains be shaken and the hills be

removed, yet my unfailing love for you will not be
shaken nor my covenant of peace be removed," says
the Lord, who has compassion on you (Isaiah 54:10).

5. *Hesed* is faithfulness in action; fixed, determined,
almost stubborn steadfastness which, in God's case,
lasts forever, and "is better than life" (Ps. 63:3). Psalm
136 with its continuing refrain: *His steadfast love
endures forever* presents *hesed* as an essential and
unchanging part of His nature. "To thee, O Lord,
belongs steadfast love," the psalmist says in Psalm
62:12. The fullness of meaning in *hesed* can only be
found in God, but because the Holy Spirit now indwells
believers, we also possess the potential to love in this
way. The choice is ours! We can operate on the basis of
our own selfish interests, always putting ourselves first,
or we can allow the greatness of His love to enlarge the
narrow capacities of our own hearts.

> Recognize that God is the true source of faith-
> fulness for your marriage, and choose to
> demonstrate His faithful *hesed* love to your
> partner. This is the eleventh step in forging a
> marriage that endures.

SUGGESTIONS

Form the B-E-S-T habit of nurturing by following these
steps:

1. In your notebook make your own list of ways to
apply each part of the prescription to your relationship.
Transfer them to 3x5 cards you can keep with you as

reminders. As you make new discoveries about what your partner desires, add them to your list.

2. Launch your new plan with strong initiative. Give your new beginning such momentum that the temptation to break down will not occur as soon as it otherwise might. Each day you continue on, you are strengthening your resolve and building for the future.

3. Never allow an exception to occur until the B-E-S-T habit is securely rooted in your life. William James says that each lapse is like dropping a ball of string which one is carefully winding up; a single slip undoes more than a great many turns will wind up again. By continuity and consistency, you will train yourself to respond rightly with less effort.

4. Take the first possible opportunity to act on each specific B-E-S-T goal you set. Concrete actions will establish your behavior as habit. When a resolve or a fine glow of feeling is allowed to evaporate without bearing practical fruit, it actually works to discourage us from making future decisions.

5. Practice every day. Do a little more than you ordinarily would to establish the habit so that when you are tempted to let up, you'll be nerved and ready to stand the test.

6. Don't let the discouragement of a "failure" cause you to quit. Instead, go back to the B-E-S-T principles and see how you can remedy the situation, and go on from that point. The idea is not to become a perfect person, but to nurture your partner in the ways that he or she needs and desires most.

7. Commit your way unto the Lord and your plans will be established.

6

INDIFFERENCE OR LOVING

Are we taking our relationship for granted, or are we learning more about each other as time goes by?

Love never fails (1 Cor. 13:8).

One of the momentous choices you will make in marriage is whether to allow indifference to set the emotional tone of your relationship, or to learn and practice the very personal art of loving your partner.

But where does indifference come from, and how can it take over a relationship? As counselors, we see that nothing is started with such high hopes and shining expectations, yet fails as often as the love which propels newlyweds into marriage. God's Word says that "love never fails." So the problem lies not with love, but with "lovers" whose choices too often are based on misconceptions, rather than the truth about love.

God Himself is Love. He communicates this truth through the Bible so that we can be free to love, but we have an enemy who attempts to destroy love by disseminating lies about it. Satan's lies, some of them quite subtle, are successfully spread like viruses throughout the world, and as a result we're likely to be infected, even while growing up. Almost all of us, without realizing it, accumulate a mixed bag of myths and misconceptions about love. Unless we learn better, we take them into marriage with us.

A wife told us, "I can see that I've been emotionally illiterate for most of my married life. And, oh, I've paid the price of ignorance!" Her husband, of course, had to pay a price in unhappiness, as well, for the false ideas about love which had dominated her behavior.

You see, what you believe about love — true or false — will always influence your behavior toward your mate. This will certainly affect your marriage and will help determine your future happiness and well-being. What you believe is that important.

For example, people who believe the world's lies about love tend to take their relationship for granted because they think love is a feeling that should happen automatically and get even better without effort on their part. Or, if the feelings stop happening, they believe nothing can be done about it anyway.

Be warned that if you don't choose to actively practice the art of loving, an emotional climate of indifference will develop almost by default. A love relationship left to itself will not improve with time; the original momentum will not continue. In fact, the principle of deterioration sets in as soon as apparent indifference opens the door. It may be only laziness, or ignorance, but the same harmful effects result. People have to work at their relationship to keep it working, and loving one's mate always requires knowledgeable effort.

In the next few pages we want to give you some truths which will help you make the best choices in your love life. These truths can revolutionize any love relationship. If you absorb them and live by them, there will be no room for Satan's deceptions, and no way they can control you. Here, in visual form, are the topics we'll be covering, beginning at the foundation and moving upward — from basic principles of love to a clear vision of the love which will keep you on a steady course throughout your married life.

A Clear View of Love

Heaven's Resources for Lovers

The Five Ways of Loving in Marriage

How Real Love Behaves: A Biblical Checklist

Basic Principles for Lovers: The Truth About Love

BASIC PRINCIPLES FOR LOVERS: THE TRUTH ABOUT LOVE

We begin with four basic principles every lover needs to know. Each principle answers and corrects a false belief commonly held about love which hinders us

from learning and practicing the art of loving our partner. It's vital to make these truths a part of your belief
system if they are not already.

1. *I can learn what love is from the Word of God. It is
rational, not irrational. I can understand love and grow in
the understanding of it throughout my lifetime.*

Contrast this truth with Satan's most subtle lie
about love: that it is a misty, uncertain, irrational thing
which we can never "get a handle on." (Rather like a
big, beautiful soap bubble!) This lie tries to diminish
our vision of love and dilute its influence upon our life
by suggesting that, since love is irrational, we can never
understand it. If we can't be sure and clear about it in
our minds, love is reduced to something as weak as
wishful thinking.

The fact is that love is the one thing in life about
which we can have a blazing certainty. There is nothing
more realistic and powerful in the history of the world
than that moment at the crossroads of time when God's
Son, Jesus Christ, died for us, so that we might live forever
in the eternal circle of His love. There is nothing more sure
than His love for us, and we too can love realistically and
powerfully "because He first loved us" (1 John 4:19).

Let us go on loving one another, for love comes from
God. Every man who truly loves is God's son and has
some knowledge of him. But the man who does not
love cannot know him at all, for God is love.

To us, the greatest demonstration of God's love for
us has been his sending his only Son into the
world to give us life through him. We see real

love, not in the fact that we loved God, but that he
loved us and sent his Son to make personal atone-
ment for our sins. If God loved us as much as that,
surely we, in our turn, should love each other!

If we love each other God does actually live within
us, and his love grows in us towards perfection
(1 John 4:7 – 12 Phillips).

In other words, if we want to learn what real love
is, we can go to the Scriptures — our only accurate
source of information about love — to discover how
God loves. Basically, we will find that love is always
drawing the beloved with loving-kindness, always *doing*
the very best for the beloved. Why? Because love recognizes the unique value of the beloved and chooses to
affirm it always. The Lord's words to His frequently
unlovely people offer the best example of this: *"Because
you are precious in My sight, and honored, and I love you,
I give"* (Isa. 43:4 AMPLIFIED). Love is a steadfast choice
consistently backed up by action — a rational choice
made with the full power of the will.

We know that real love is always rational, consistent, purposeful, and creative because God, who *is*
Love, is also the One whose wisdom created and main-
tains the world. Think of it! All the incredibly diverse
life forms of our world and all the heavenly bodies in
the galaxies of space with their majestic, mathematical
order have been conceived and kept in motion by the
God of love. Love makes sense. The principles of love
can be understood and lived by, just as seafaring men
can find their way across trackless oceans by the fixed
positions of the stars.

2. *Love is neither easy nor simple. It is an art that I must want to learn and pour my life into.*

Although real love can be understood, it does not come easily or automatically. This fact answers the common misconception among young people that love is the simplest thing in the world, that it's easy to love, requiring neither thought nor effort. No one has to learn about love or even think about it — it's just a matter of doing what comes naturally! With this lie, Satan tries to cheapen love.

The fact is that if you do what comes naturally, you'll be wrong almost every time. By nature we human beings are selfish, not generous. True love demands a generosity of spirit and life which gives gladly and freely for the benefit of the beloved — and keeps on giving. Real love costs! It will require much from you even when the giving is pure joy.

You can't become a skilled lover by treating love as a pleasure you dabble in when you're in the mood. The art of loving must be learned as a discipline just like the art of music, or medicine, or any other work which requires the most skilled craftsmanship and mastery of technique. You must want to learn this art so much that you are willing to pour your time and strength into the process. You can become an expert lover if you will put forth the effort to learn what you need to know about the art of loving, and practice it on a daily basis. We're recommending action, not just theoretical knowledge. As the language experts point out, Science *knows;* art *does.*

3. *Love is an active power that I control by my own will. I am not the helpless slave of love. I can choose to love.*

Most of the man-meets-woman, man-loses-woman plots of films and television come from the premise that love is a feeling that just happens. Or else it doesn't happen. Or it happens and then stops happening so that nothing can be done to recapture that feeling, once it goes.

The truth is that love is an active power which you were meant to control by your own will. You are not "just a prisoner of love" as the song claims. If you are a Christian with the love of God in your heart, you can choose to love your marriage partner moment by moment, no matter what the circumstances are, or how you are feeling. (Remember that you are *more* than your emotions.)

4. *Love is the power that will produce love as I learn to give it rather than strain to attract it.*

Most people today worry about finding someone to love them and keep on loving them. Advertising plays on those worries by sending the message that people have to learn how to be desirable in order to be loved and to hold on to their lover. This means choosing the right toothpaste, perfume, shaving cream, shampoo, deodorant — the list of products almost guaranteed to bring love into your life is endless.

But not everything can be blamed on television commercials. Our media-oriented society unashamedly measures desirability by three flimsy yardsticks: popularity, sex appeal, and great looks. (It also helps to have a rising career and the income for an exciting life-style.) But although people may be paying more attention to their appearance, taking more exotic vacations, earning

more money, and becoming more knowledgeable about
sex than ever before — their longing for someone to
love them, really love them, has not abated in the least.
With the rising divorce rate, people are even more
lonely, and more desperate for a love relationship based
on reality.

The Bible holds the secret. It can show you how to
be so lovable and desirable that your marriage partner
will adore you and never let you go. The secret involves
learning to give love rather than straining and striving
to attract it — a powerful secret which only a few people know. One word of caution: Many mistakes are
made in the name of love. You must learn how to love
in ways that correspond to your partner's own measure-
ment of love. What will make your mate *feel* loved by
you? When you become skilled at the art of loving, you
will know the answer.

HOW REAL LOVE BEHAVES: A BIBLICAL CHECKLIST

Here is another dimension of learning to love (and thus
becoming the most desirable of marriage partners). We
need to learn the characteristics of true love and let
those become our pattern of behavior to follow. One
passage of Scripture holds a mirror before our eyes so
that we can compare how we love with the way real
love thinks, speaks, and behaves, especially when
tested. And tested we will be!

So toss out your unrealistic expectations and
accept the fact that you will be tested all too frequently while you are learning to adapt to one
another in marriage. As the process goes on, don't be

surprised if marriage magnifies every flaw in your disposition while self-centeredness is being replaced by real love.

The truth of 1 Corinthians 13, given here in chart form, can help. Study it, pray over it, live with it until its influence transforms your behavior, especially toward your mate.

WHAT LOVE IS AND IS NOT:
THE DEFINITIVE STATEMENT
As found in 1 Corinthians 13

Love is . . .	Love is not . . .
1. patient, long-tempered	impatient, short with others
2. kind, gracious, good	unkind, indifferent
3. glad when good things happen to others	envious, jealous
4. modest, undemanding	a show-off, a bragger
5. humble, seeing itself realistically	haughty, conceited, proud
6. polite, courteous	rude, apt to behave badly
7. more concerned with the well-being of others than its own welfare	selfish, self-centered, always insisting on its own way
8. even-tempered	touchy, irritable, easily annoyed

Love does . . .	Love does not . . .
1. overlook grievances	keep score of wrongs, nurture grudges
2. rejoice with the truth, become happy when truth is honored	rejoice at unrighteousness, feel good when things go badly for others
3. bear up under anything and everything	give up on others and drag the worst out into the open for others to gloat over
4. believe all things, give others the benefit of the doubt	believe the worst about others
5. hope all things under all circumstances	accept failure as the last word
6. endure all things without weakening	give up, admit defeat

THERE IS NOTHING GREATER THAN LOVE!

THE FIVE WAYS OF LOVING IN MARRIAGE

Loving one another requires "know-how" as well as consistent effort. But our English word *love* is an overworked and inadequate term for someone who wants to know *how* to love. The word has been used in so many meaningless ways that authors feel the need to qualify it when they want to say something important. For instance, the poet Edgar Allan Poe wrote, "We loved with a love that was more than love." And in a currently acclaimed television fantasy, the Beauty and the Beast describe their profound caring for one another as "a bond stronger than love."

When we developed the *love life* principles for thousands of couples who wanted to rekindle love in their marriage, we went back to the precise language of the Greek New Testament along with some vibrant Hebrew terms of the Old Testament to distinguish and describe the various aspects of love and to explain how they could enrich a marriage. We will give you these five ways of loving now, not as a language exercise, but as a practical explanation of what your marriage can be when love finds its full expression in your relationship. (Refer back to chapter 5 for the sixth way of loving, the steadfast loving-kindness called *hesed.*)

Please understand that we're not suggesting window shopping. You can't major on one kind of loving and discard another. Each builds on the other. Each has its own special place, as you will find when you put them into practice, and yet all are interrelated.

We'll briefly describe each facet of love, then give you guidelines on experiencing its delights in your relationship. Pay special attention to the key words!

1. Epithumia — Sexual Desire

Thy **desire** shall be toward thy husband (Gen. 3:16, KJV).

I am my beloved's and his **desire** is for me (Song 7:10).

This facet of love — a strong craving and physiological desire — is suggested by a Greek word which the Bible never calls love. However, it describes a crucial aspect of the love affair between husband and wife. *Epithumia* is a strong desire of any kind — sometimes good, sometimes bad. It means to set the heart on, to long for, rightly or wrongly. When used in the Bible in a negative way, it is translated lust. When used in a positive way, it is translated *desire,* and this is the meaning we refer to. In marriage, husband and wife should have a strong physical desire for each other that expresses itself in pleasurable sexual lovemaking.

HOW TO LOVE YOUR PARTNER SEXUALLY

a. You need complete, accurate medical information.
b. You need to understand sex from the biblical perspective.
c. You need to develop the right approach in your marriage:
  • by eliminating the negatives, avoiding all criticism.
  • by building a series of enjoyable physical experiences together based on physical touching and emotional closeness.

The Key Words: INTIMACY and RESPONSE

2. Eros — Romantic Love

Let him kiss me with the kisses of his mouth: For thy **love** is better than wine (Song 1:2, KJV).

This way of loving — literally, to boil — never appears in the New Testament, but its Hebrew counterpart is used in the Old Testament. *Eros,* more than any other kind of love, carries with it the idea of romance. *Eros* is not always sensual, but it includes the idea of yearning to unite with and the desire to possess the beloved. Romantic, passionate, and sentimental — this love often provides the starting point for marriage. It has been called rapture; exquisite pleasure; a strong, sweet, and sometimes terrifying emotion because it is so all-absorbing. At its best, romantic love is pure and beautiful and ennobling, and will add all manner of delights to your marriage.

It's important to remember that *eros* is always "the love of the worthy." When a young man or a young woman falls in love, it is always because the beloved is perceived as attractive. How you *see* each other will determine the quality of *eros* in your marriage in the months and years ahead.

HOW TO BUILD ROMANTIC LOVE

A. Eros love is a pleasurable learned response to:
 • the way your partner looks and feels,
 • the things your partner says and does,
 • the emotional experiences you share.
B. Think about all these ways your mate pleases you.
 • Use your God-given gift of imagination to build this love in your mind.
 • Never allow criticism or ridicule of your mate to enter the picture.
C. Remember — you are teaching your mate to

respond to you all the time, either positively or
negatively. So send out pleasant and pleasurable signals.

• Provide the right emotional climate for your
  mate to experience romantic feelings.

• Provide the physical stimulus of closeness,
  touching, eye contact.

• Set up the conditions in which your partner
  will find it easy to love you.

The Key Words: PLEASURE and ROMANCE

3. Storge — Natural Affection

Be **kindly affectioned** one to another with
brotherly love, in honor preferring one another
(Rom. 12:10, KJV).

This term represents the natural affection of marriage, a warm, devoted loyalty which you feel and show
to one another because you *belong*. It's such an unspec-
tacular, down-to-earth love, its importance may be
underestimated. But listen to this report (quoted in our
book *Love Life*) from a couple who developed *storge*
love early in their marriage. They've been together more
than thirty years now, but here's what *storge* meant to
their relationship during what they look back on as the
"rocky years."

"On the way to our June wedding, we thought we
had everything going for us. Our friendship was warm,
our romantic feelings even warmer, and, as for the fires
of passion, they were just waiting for the match! After
we settled into married life, the companionship and

sexual desire and romantic thrills were still there. But it was all a little less perfect than we had expected because we were such imperfect people. The pink glow of romance hadn't prepared us for that! We weren't Christians then, so we didn't know that *agape* love could glue us together.

"Fortunately, something else brought us through those first rocky years when wedded bliss almost got buried under the unbliss. You might call what developed between us a sense of belonging. We had decided right from the start that it was us against the world — two people forming a majority of one. So whatever happened, or however much we clashed in private, we stuck by each other. We were like a brother and sister on the playground. We might scrap with each other, but let an outsider try to horn in and he had to take us both on! If one of us hurt, the other wiped away the tears. We made a habit of believing in each other while our careers got off the ground.

"We showed each other all the kindness that two impatient young people could be expected to show — and then some more. It really wasn't long until we discovered something stupendous about our relationship: We found out we belonged. We came first with each other, and always would. Because we belonged to each other, no one could spoil our love and togetherness from the outside. Only we could do that, and we weren't about to! It was too good to lose. A lot of people seem to spend their whole life looking for a feeling of belonging. Maybe they don't know that marriage is the best place to find it."

This facet of love we call *belonging* is essential to your happiness in marriage. We all need an atmosphere at home which is secure, where we feel completely comfortable with one another, knowing that we belong there, and that our happiness and well-being are supremely important to our partner. Here's how to turn your marriage into a place of *homecoming* for both of you.

HOW TO GIVE THE GIFT OF BELONGING

A. Establish the viewpoint of oneness in your marriage.
- •Do not see yourselves separately.
- •Refuse to let pressures divide you.
- •Be loyal to each other under all circumstances.

B. Reinforce your sense of family solidarity.
- •Spend comfortable time together.
- •Always be supportive and kind.
- •Show your partner you can be counted on.

The Key Words: RELIABILITY and KINDNESS

4. Phileo — Friendship Love

That they may teach the young women to . . . **love** (phileo) their husbands (Titus 2:4, KJV).

Phileo is the love one feels for a cherished friend of either sex. Jesus had this love for a disciple: "One of His disciples whom Jesus loved — whom He esteemed and delighted in . . ." (John 13:23 AMPLIFIED). Peter expressed his *phileo* love for Jesus: "Lord . . . You know that I love You — that I have a deep, instinctive, personal affection for You, as for a close friend. . . ." (John

21:17 AMPLIFIED). And Jonathan and David provide an Old Testament example: "The soul of Jonathan was knit with the soul of David, and Jonathan loved him as his own soul" (1 Sam. 18:1, KJV).

This same *phileo* is the cherishing love of marriage. It takes on added intensity and enjoyment as part of the love bond of husband and wife. When two people in marriage share themselves — their lives and all that they are — they develop this love of mutual affection, rapport, and comradeship. They become best friends, delighting in one another's company, and caring for each other tenderly. None of the loves of marriage offers more consistent pleasure than *phileo*. The camaraderie of best friends who are also lovers seems twice as exciting and doubly precious. As you put your energies to building and maintaining this love in your marriage, remember two important things. First, sharing is the key that unlocks the emotions of friendship. Second, the conditions you set up in your marriage must be conducive to friendship. Through personal experience you already know how to make and keep friends. Now it's a matter of applying what you know to build this most important friendship of your life.

HOW TO BECOME BEST FRIENDS

A. By genuine togetherness.
- Spend quality time together.
- Focus your attention on each other.
- Share your activities and interests.

B. By developing real communication.
- Share your thoughts, goals, ideals.

•Develop a safe atmosphere in which you can share inmost feelings, and totally be yourself.

The Key Words: COMRADESHIP, RAPPORT, and REVELATION

5. Agape — Unconditional Love

God commendeth his love toward us in that, while we were yet sinners, Christ died for us (Rom. 5:8, KJV).

Agape is the love so often spoken of in the New Testament because it is God's love. *Agape* is that showering of grace and favor which transforms our life; of unshakable commitment and unselfish giving; of great kindness and concern for our highest welfare; of unconditional acceptance as though arms were open always to receive us, no matter what. Everyone wants and desperately needs this unconditional love. But it cannot be purchased; it cannot even be earned by good behavior. God is the *source*, and until we understand this we will be unable to love each other in marriage with the love that brings every good thing into our lives.

As you learn to give this priceless gift to one another you will find that there is no substitute for the emotional well-being that comes from feeling loved and accepted, completely, unconditionally, and permanently.

HOW TO LOVE THE AGAPE WAY

A. Choose with your will to love unconditionally and permanently.

B. Ask God to enable you to love with His love.

C. Develop the biblical and personal knowledge of your partner's needs and how to meet them. If the loving actions of *agape* are not guided by precise knowledge of your partner, they will miss the mark.

D. Apply everything you know in communicating this love. Agape love is an action word: always doing the best for the object of your love.

E. Give your partner what he or she needs most: the assurance of being
• totally accepted.
•permanently loved.

The Key Word: GIVING (based on knowledge)

HEAVEN'S RESOURCES FOR LOVERS

This conversation was reported to us recently. Young granddaughter: "Grandma, I don't think I'm going to get married when I grow up." Grandma: "Why is that, Kristy?" Child: "Because I don't want to be divorced."

Children have a way of going to the heart of the matter. For this little girl and thousands like her, divorce does seem to be a natural consequence of marriage — the second part of the story, the unhappy ending.

But here are some facts to count on, facts which more than balance today's dark statistics. These truths give solid reassurance of God's readiness to help you build the kind of marriage that happily lasts a lifetime.

1. It is God's will in every marriage that the couple love each other with an absorbing spiritual, emotional, and physical attraction that continues to grow throughout their lifetime together.

2. God is the one who made you, who thought up the idea of marriage and ordained it for your blessing, and who gives you the capacity to love. He is the One who knows best how to build love into your particular relationship. You can trust Him to be intimately involved in your efforts to develop a love-filled marriage.

3. It is possible for any Christian couple to develop this love relationship in their marriage because it is in harmony with God's express will.

If the time should come when you feel the temporary urge to "give up," refresh yourself with these truths. Remember that heaven's resources are at your disposal. Any couple who wants and chooses to build a love-filled marriage *can* do so.

A CLEAR VIEW OF LOVE

No matter how long we study *love*, we find that our vision is still too small!

In the beautiful little book, *Hinds' Feet on High Places,* which tells of the climb to the High Places of Love, the heroine and her friends reach "the beginners" slopes and realize how much more lies beyond. They see that there are ranges upon ranges which they had not even dreamt of while they were still down in the valleys with their limited views.

The thirteenth chapter of 1 Corinthians, which we considered earlier, gives us a hint of these "ranges upon ranges" of which we know nothing yet. But we do know this much: Love is the most important thing in the world. There is nothing that matters more than love. Love is stronger than death itself. There is nothing more powerful than love. Love is the only thing that lasts, the only thing that will endure forever. There is nothing as permanent as love.

We trust that these truths will be a launching pad for your own discoveries.

> Decide to pour your life into learning the art of loving your mate, and avoiding any hint of indifference. This is the twelfth step in establishing a happy marriage.

SUGGESTIONS

This chapter contains the core information you need to learn the art of loving and practice it. What will you do with it?

1. Think about your marriage at this point. Would you describe the emotional atmosphere as loving or indifferent? How have you contributed to this climate? Do you feel a change is needed? If you continue moving in the direction you're now going, will you be pleased with the outcome?

2. Consider making a definite decision to commit

yourself to the art of loving your mate, for out of this decision will flow all the small secret choices which characterize your life together. A decision is a signal that you have made up your mind. The word *decision* literally means "a cutting short." It indicates a cutting short of uncertainty and sets the stage for action. Record what you decide in your notebook.

3. Use the five ways of loving as a checklist to determine where your marriage needs extra attention. Based on the information in this section, plan some specific ways to enhance your relationship.

PART THREE

HOW WELL IS YOUR PARTNERSHIP
WORKING?

7

IN CONFLICT: CHOICES THAT MAKE YOU A WINNING TEAM

> How well do we handle the conflicts which inevitably arise when two human beings try to build one life together?

"Live together in harmony, live together in love, as though you had only one mind and one spirit between you. Never act from motives of rivalry or personal vanity, but in humility think more of one another than you do of yourselves" (Phil. 2:2 – 3 Phillips).

It's been said that marriage presents one of the most difficult personal problems in life, because the most emotional and romantic of all human dreams has to be consolidated into an ordinary working relationship.

Many of us would agree. And yet the statement is not precisely true, for marriage is no ordinary relationship. God designed it to be the ideal *partnership* in which each partner supports and complements the other; a partnership which is continually renewed and refreshed by the presence and power of love.

Still, marriage, (though far from ordinary) is very much a *working* relationship. Reverse the comfortable myth that says "If two people love each other, everything will work out," and it becomes truth: *If two people want to keep on loving each other, they will need to work out everything!* An enormous difference of approach lies between these two ideas. By inspecting your secret choices in marriage, you can see which statement you actually believe and which approach you have been taking.

Every married couple faces the same challenge: how to create a good partnership. The success of your marriage may well turn on this point. Since marriage is not an endless romantic encounter, but a sharing of life as it really is — the problems as well as the joys; the routine responsibilities as well as the rewards — nothing can take the place of your ability to function happily and effectively as a team. And this never happens without a great deal of understanding and effort.

The roadblock which most couples encounter almost immediately could be labeled, simply, *conflict*. Some couples try to pretend it's not there, and thus make no progress at all. Some attempt to detour the long way around, only to find that they can't avoid it. And others keep smashing into it and retreating, dazed and wounded, to make another run! There's only one adequate way to deal with this barricade: It must be removed (stone by stone, if necessary), and that takes teamwork. It's a hard fact of marriage that your partnership will never work well unless the two of you learn to work together in resolving the hundreds of conflicts that arise whenever two human beings try to build one life. How you approach conflict and how well you learn to manage it will be key factors in determining the course of your marriage. Here are some suggestions which can help.

HOW TO APPROACH THE CONFLICTS IN YOUR MARRIAGE

1. *Approach conflicts with acceptance.*

Accept conflicts, especially in the early years, as a normal and potentially useful part of marriage. Granted, they may come as an unpleasant surprise on the honeymoon or soon after. Dating, no matter how frequent, is never the same as living together constantly. We think we know our loved one at the time we say "I do," but human beings are so complex that it takes years for us to begin to understand one another well.

Conflicts, though painful, nudge us into adjusting our expectations and needs to harmonize with those of our marriage partner. Because of the fall of man and our inheritance of a sinful nature, the process of two learning to become one frequently includes conflict. How much, and how painful, will depend on whether we respond in biblical ways and follow biblical counsel in building our marriages. When the red light of conflict clicks on, we can be thankful for the warning signal which shows us an area of our relationship that needs attention. If we allow them to, conflicts can motivate us to build a stronger marriage, and if we are sensitive to the issues, we will learn more precisely how to please one another — always a prerequisite to a happier marriage.

Just as we must accept the reality of conflict in

our marriage, we also need to accept our marriage partner, even while the disagreement is raging. Marriage seems to act as a magnifying glass, emphasizing our every imperfection, and nowhere is the view in the glass quite as grim as during a quarrel when anger momentarily distorts our vision. This is our great opportunity to choose to grant our lover the gift of unconditional love; to see him or her without the flaws. Acceptance also neutralizes the possibility of harmful aftereffects when the clash is over and the matter has been resolved.

2. *Approach conflicts with a perspective of oneness.*

Approach conflicts in your marriage with a viewpoint that eliminates much of the sting and keeps the positive juices flowing, even while the flak is flying. In short, keep sight of yourselves as the insiders, and this conflict as an intruder with no right to control your relationship. It's a matter of perspective. If you begin to see yourselves as two adversaries, engaged in open warfare or sniper attacks, you have reason to be dismayed, because you are, in reality, *one flesh*. If you turn on each other to retaliate, it is like trying to retaliate against yourself. Always remember that you and your mate are not enemies. The quarrels pose the threat, for they can bring deadly harm to your marriage if not controlled. How much better to approach conflicts as two people who belong together — an indivisible unit — and who refuse to let anything come between them.

The Scriptures counsel us to live together as though we shared one mind and one spirit. Not possible, you say? As believers, indwelt by the Holy Spirit and guided by the Scriptures, it is wholly possible to develop this oneness of approach and remain united even while confronting and resolving our differences.

And so we need to view ourselves as one, to seek oneness of mind and spirit, and to act as one against that conflict which threatens to divide us. If we maintain our sense of unity, neither helplessness ("What can I do?") nor hopelessness ("What's the use?") can ever defeat us.

3. *Approach conflict with established guidelines*.

We have already suggested the need for biblical counsel in times of conflict. But how about preparing for it ahead of time by establishing in your mind some guidelines to direct your choices? The biblical guidelines suggested in Philippians 2 are harmony and love: "live together in harmony; live together in love. . . ." The hope of harmony will not settle every difference of opinion in marriage, but the standard of harmony can modify your behavior while you are dealing with the problem at hand. The yardstick of love, as found in 1 Corinthians 13 (see chapter 6), provides the perfect model of behavior and attitude. Let this shape your choices, and you will have nothing to fear from the times of adjustment in your marriage.

4. *Approach conflict with commitment to teamwork*.

Up to this point we have used the illustration of warfare, because our disagreements in marriage often seem more like battles than anything else. But the unique partnership of marriage requires strong teamwork, and that image can also add to our understanding of how to approach conflicts.

If your differences in marriage were a game to be

won or lost, how would it usually go in your relationship? Think about it. When you have a conflict about something — anything, large or small — what often happens? Does one of you "win" most of the time while the other usually backs down or gives in?

What does winning really consist of? Having the last word? Convincing the other to change? Talking the loudest or pouting the longest? Is it a reluctant submission by one of you in order to keep your relationship intact? Would one or both of you rather be *right* at the other's expense, than be in harmony? Do you get your own way by applying some sort of pressure? Is winning your way more important than your partner's happiness or the well-being of your marriage?

Winning, as we've already suggested, can mean something else entirely. It doesn't have to be a contest with the two of you pitted against one another, one winning, one losing. It can be a *win-win* approach where you join together as a team in resolving the problem rather than "playing against" one another. If you handle the conflict in such a way that your love and commitment are actually strengthened by the solution you find together, you both come out the clear winners.

It's important to see yourselves, not as competitors against one another, but as co-laborers in the field of marriage. The Bible cautions against "motives of rivalry or personal vanity." We know that when members of a team begin competing with one another, the team's "win" statistics usually take a plunge. In marriage, such rivalry chips away at the peace of the home. The effects of personal vanity are even worse, for a narcissistic person, once offended, can easily switch from "love" to hatred and a thirst for revenge.

Pride, that ferocious refusal to bend an inch, is the most common obstacle to the resolution of quarrels and the healing that forgiveness can bring. It's also the thing that God hates most, according to the Bible. "God opposes the proud, but gives grace to the humble," warns the proverb, quoted twice in the New Testament (James 4:6 and 1 Peter 5:5).

In contrast, humility can bless your marriage by applying the sweet oil of harmony to every point of friction in your relationship. As the saying goes, "The cure for conflict is a humble spirit." How does humility behave? Unassumingly. Unconcerned with status because it does not have to compensate for insecurity. Not self-occupied. It accepts what God has done and what He has given, and does not go to extremes by putting itself up or down. Humility, by biblical definition, considers others better than itself, and looks after the interests of others as well as its own concerns. (See Phil. 2:3 – 11.) Humility may sound like a foreign term to a generation raised on the benefits of self-fulfillment and assertiveness training, but remember that it is our Creator's prescription for harmony and peace in human relationships. He has given us the living example of strength with humility in the person of the Lord Jesus Christ.

5. *Approach conflict as a crucial test.*

How you handle your conflicts will be a crucial test of your partnership. Much hangs in the balance. The survival of your marriage may even be at risk, for the manner in which couples handle their disagreements has a strong impact on both the *quality* and the *stability* of their marriage.

In the olden days when divorce was rarely granted, Queen Elizabeth I of England complained to the churches: "How few matrimonies there be without chidings, brawlings, tauntings, bitter cursings, and fightings." People suffered but remained married.

Today, in a society brought up with the idea of "instant relief," only those strongly committed to marriage are willing to put up with the "chidings, brawlings, tauntings" and so on. Even a temporarily strained relationship is apt to be written off the way an interviewer summed up the broken marriage of a famous television personality and her husband. "They had great times," the writer blithely said, "and then the great times were over and it was time to take separate paths."

Married couples today tend to give themselves too little time to adjust to one another and to make the changes which may be necessary in order to build a good marriage. Patience has never been in shorter supply. That's why it is essential for couples to learn and practice the skills which can enable them to understand their conflicts and work them through satisfactorily.

6. *Approach conflict with confidence that it can benefit your marriage.*

If we learn to handle conflict so that we encourage and build one another up rather than tearing each other down, we can find the experience beneficial. Think of it as a means of increasing your closeness, for if you manage your differences effectively, the result will be a deeper intimacy to bless your marriage.

In our marital partnership we have the privilege of creating many things — conceiving and rearing children; forming a life together, building a home, shaping a loving environment for others to enjoy; pouring our energies into work or a ministry which we can share; creating and sharing experiences of beauty; and providing a role model to help others who are looking for examples of steadfast love between husband and wife. Doing away with the barriers of conflict by moving the stumbling blocks out of the way, one by one as they appear, is another constructive work which we can give ourselves to with joy.

We can never take happiness in marriage for granted, as something owed to us. The Arabian Nights fantasy, *The Thief of Bagdad,* a spectacular silent film of 1924, which was restored and revived on PBS, ends with a subtitle on the screen lest anyone miss the point: "Happiness must be earned." Even the magic of the Arabian Nights was not enough to ensure happiness for the lovers. Happiness — then and now — must be earned by our behavior and attitudes: by our sacrifice, courage, endurance, and patience; and by our secret choices.

HOW TO MANAGE THE CONFLICTS IN YOUR MARRIAGE

We've discussed the best ways to approach conflict when it appears. Now we want to suggest three ways to manage it constructively and resolve it satisfactorily.

1. *Analyze the situation.*

   This requires some objectivity, but it's an essential part of the problem-solving process. Your purpose is to discover what each of you are doing to set off the quarrels, and how you contribute to their escalation. Recognize that you have a strong influence on one another, and share the responsibility for what's happening. Note what triggers the disagreement and how each of you responds. Be very specific.

For instance, one couple made a valuable discovery when the wife realized that issues were not the problem. It was her husband's practice of raising his voice (she called it "yelling") which made her feel attacked. In response, she became defensive and resentful, and soon they were off in a spate of ill feelings that had little to do with the subject they were discussing. The husband discovered that raising his voice at certain times was nothing more than a bad habit learned from his father many years before, and that it had small significance — except to trigger a hundred unnecessary confrontations.

Another wife found that although she had always perceived herself as the "victim," in reality her complaints, voiced in a weak, self-pitying manner, were setting off explosions of frustration in her husband. When she recognized her own power of choice and took equal responsibility for the problems in their life, they were able to establish new, productive ways of interacting.

It's especially important to note clashing patterns of behavior which the two of you have unconsciously picked up from your families. One of your primary tasks in the critical first year of marriage is to work your way out of these behavior patterns and to develop a new style which represents the way you want to live together. It takes time to unlearn behaviors, but the process will speed up when you decide on positive ways to replace the undesirable behavior patterns, and put them into practice.

When couples can freely discuss their family homes and analyze the behaviors and customs they admire and want to retain, and also agree on the destructive behaviors and practices they want to abolish, they eliminate many of the controversies of marriage. This detachment from families of origin and the couple's choice to see themselves as a new decision-making unit is a key factor in building a marriage that lasts.

Your analysis should include the topics you fight about. Is there one issue that comes up frequently and is never resolved? Money? Personal habits? Sex? Child rearing? In-law problems? Or do you quarrel constantly about anything and everything? If so, the chances are good that you are substituting irrelevant issues for a problem or problems you have not yet confronted. Is there hurt so deep within that it has never been exposed to healing? Is there a topic on which you are unable to communicate? Is there a sense of anger or outrage which you can scarcely explain yourself?

In some cases, your problems may go deeper than the ordinary conflicts of marriage which we are considering here. After reading the next chapter, "Power Struggles: The Secret War," if you still feel confused about what is happening in your relationship, we encourage you to consult a biblical counselor who can help you to understand your conflicts and resolve them.

Finally, analyze how you are handling your conflicts. By pretending they aren't there? By trying to avoid them through elaborate means which only make you angrier inside? Or by living on the treadmill of love/anger cycles where you are first alienated, then reconciled, only to go through the process again and again, never dealing with the underlying causes of the quarrel? Peace at the expense of truth will never last, because the disruptive factor has not been removed, and it will return to strike again.

It's been estimated that only one couple in five knows how to move in the direction of lasting peace and harmony. Most, if not all, of these couples are the fortunate ones who know how to apply biblical principles in resolving and healing conflicts.

2. *Apply biblical principles.*

The Bible addresses these principles to believers. It is not that they will not work for all people, but that people will find them difficult to live out over a period of time without the power of the indwelling Holy Spirit. The fourth chapter of Ephesians explains that believers can apply these truths because they have been made new in their mental attitudes. They are no longer empty in their thinking, darkened in their understanding, and ignorant of the true state of affairs. Here are seven principles from Ephesians 4 which will prove invaluable in managing the conflicts of married life.

(1) IN YOUR ANGER DO NOT SIN (V. 26).

Anger is only a human emotion — raw material — which can be directed in good ways or bad. God does not command feelings, but He instructs us how to behave, no matter what our feelings are. It is possible to be legitimately angry without sinning, but it will require the greatest care and attention to following the rest of the counsel in this passage.

(2) DO NOT LET THE SUN GO DOWN WHILE YOU ARE STILL ANGRY, AND DO NOT GIVE THE DEVIL A FOOTHOLD (vv. 26, 27).

The enemy of our souls looks for a place to stand nearby, to find even the smallest piece of territory he can claim in our lives. He would like to use our momentary anger to lead us into sin where our anger will seize control of us. But he cannot succeed in this if we "keep short accounts." This means, in marriage, that we do not "call it a day" until we have resolved our conflict and reconciled. We may not be able to work out every detail of the right way to handle the issue in the future, but our anger should be dispelled, our hearts forgiving and forgiven, and our spirits reconciled before we go to bed, preferably lying close to one another as we fall asleep.

The wisdom of this counsel is obvious to therapists who deal continually with embittered people, choked by old resentments which were never dealt with. To become angry is part of the human condition. To nurture the anger in your heart — to allow it to take up permanent residence — is sin.

(3) DO NOT LET ANY UNWHOLESOME TALK COME OUT OF YOUR MOUTHS, BUT ONLY WHAT IS HELPFUL FOR BUILDING OTHERS UP ACCORDING TO THEIR NEEDS, THAT IT MAY BENEFIT THOSE WHO LISTEN (v. 29).

It is also sin to express your exasperation, fury, or indignation in foul words or cruel speech which tears down the listener. When conflict arises, restrain your tongue, and do not speak until you can say healing, helpful, upbuilding, and beneficial things to your mate.

Good counsel can be found in Proverbs, where we are reminded that "A fool's wrath is quickly and openly known; but a prudent man ignores an insult" (Prov. 12:16 AMPLIFIED). "Good sense makes a man restrain his anger, and it is his glory to overlook a transgression or an offense" (Prov. 19:11 AMPLIFIED). "He who foams up quickly and flies into a passion will deal foolishly" (Prov. 14:17 AMPLIFIED), but "A gentle tongue (with its healing power) is a tree of life" (Prov. 15:4 AMPLIFIED). It's a wise practice to pray the prayer of the psalmist when you feel anger coming on: "Set a guard over my mouth, O Lord; keep watch over the door of my lips" (Ps. 141:3).

(4) AND DO NOT GRIEVE THE HOLY SPIRIT OF GOD, WITH WHOM YOU WERE SEALED FOR THE DAY OF REDEMPTION (V. 30).

How do we know what will offend or sadden the Holy Spirit who indwells us? We need to become intimately acquainted with the Word of God which tells us and shows us in a myriad of ways what will please and displease the Lord. This should become our standard of behavior, particularly when we are tested by the heat of anger. We should allow the Spirit of Christ to be the umpire in our hearts whenever differences and conflicts arise between us.

(5) GET RID OF ALL BITTERNESS, RAGE AND ANGER, BRAWLING AND SLANDER, ALONG WITH EVERY FORM OF MALICE (V. 31).

In these seventeen words six dangerous and disagreeable manifestations of anger and conflict are catalogued: bitterness — that ugly build-up of old anger turned inward; rage — anger expressed in outbursts; settled feelings of anger — animosity; brawling — shouting, clamor, or contention; slander — abusive evil-speaking; and malice — an active ill-will which demonstrates its spite in various kinds of wickedness and injury. We are told: Get rid of them! Remember, the choice is ours, and God will work within us, if we allow Him, both to will the right choices, and to give us the power to carry them out.

(6) BE KIND AND COMPASSIONATE TO ONE ANOTHER, FORGIVING EACH OTHER, JUST AS IN CHRIST GOD FORGAVE YOU (V. 32).

This is the positive behavior designed to replace the vices of anger listed above. First we are to be kind, even in the midst of conflict. The word means, literally, "what is suitable or fitting to a need." Be and do what is suitable and what your loved one needs. It is more than attitude; it is action. Second, we are to be compassionate, looking on our mate with a deep-seated emotional concern and affectionate sympathy. The word involves strong feelings and an empathy with our mate in what he or she is going through. Third, we are to be forgiving. This word means to give freely and graciously as a favor. What we give is a promise to lift the burden of our partner's guilt and to remember it no more. Individuals who use their spouse's past wrongdoings like a cattle prod to keep the erring one in line evidently have not yet experienced the free and gracious forgiveness available to them in Christ Jesus.

When you are attempting to communicate and negotiate differences with your mate, begin with mutual confession of wrongs and forgiveness, freely given. If you do not do this, your discussion will never get beyond replays of old offenses. Clear the air and begin afresh with the grace of forgiveness.

(7) BE IMITATORS OF GOD, THEREFORE, AS DEARLY LOVED CHILDREN AND LIVE A LIFE OF LOVE, JUST AS CHRIST LOVED US AND GAVE HIMSELF UP FOR US AS A FRAGRANT OFFERING AND SACRIFICE TO GOD (EPH. 5:1 – 2).

The counsel is simple and all-encompassing: Follow God's example through the life of His Son, just as children who are loved imitate their father gladly. Live a life of love with your marriage partner, giving yourselves freely to one another, and differences can be resolved as quietly as they arise.

3. *Adapt to one another*.

Listen to the experience of a couple who have been married twenty years. According to the husband, "We negotiated — but not without hassle, a lot of conflict, and accommodation. Looking back, we concluded that it was our ability to meet conflict head on, and not to avoid it, to utilize it as a means of becoming closer instead of permitting it to drive us apart, that enriched our relationship."

What this couple accomplished is the challenge of every married couple — to learn to adapt when differences arise (after all, no two people are going to have the same needs, desires, moods, preferences, hang-ups, or beliefs all of the time); to adjust to changing conditions; and to grow together while resolving the conflicts of their shared life.

To accomplish these tasks, a couple has to learn to negotiate, accommodate, communicate, and tolerate.

Moreover, they must learn to investigate problems in their marriage and create solutions, and, always, to demonstrate certain positive ways of relating to one another.

To negotiate is, very simply, *to talk over and arrange terms*. It also means *to solve a problem or surmount a difficulty so as to be able to proceed toward something*. This is precisely what we must do in marriage, with the goal of overcoming our conflicts and differences and proceeding together toward a harmonious, smooth-working, enjoyable partnership.

Negotiation can accomplish little without accommodation at its side. To accommodate is *to make suitable, to bring to harmony or agreement, to become adjusted and adapted, to settle differences*. We can only arrange the terms of negotiation by being willing to fit ourselves to one another's needs and wishes in marriage. Always, the goal as we negotiate is to find that proper fit together, so that we can become suitable for one another in the details and choices of our common life.

We negotiate and accommodate just as the couple married twenty years did — by refusing to allow conflicts to take control of our marriage. Instead, we confront them and utilize them to become closer and to forge deeper understanding and a stronger partnership.

But to negotiate effectively and accommodate ourselves to one another, we must learn to communicate. Although this is not a chapter on communication (see chapter 5, "Communicating: Your Lifeline in Marriage" in our book *The First Years of Forever*), here are some suggestions.

First, avoid sweeping statements and broad gener-

alizations as though they were poison to your relationship. They are! Instead, be positive and be specific.
Pinpoint changes which you would like to see, item by
item, rather than heaping clouds of general disapproval
on your partner. At the same time communicate your
respect and appreciation for your partner in every discussion. Remember that negative statements will leave
conflicts unresolved and even intensify them. Many
couples do not know how to express their needs in a
nonblaming way, but like any other skill, this can be
learned. Speak carefully, clearly, and always in a non-
attacking way. Listen as carefully as you speak, and
make sure you have the message. Take turns and don't
interrupt.

It's important to discuss these matters in a calm,
private environment. Approach the negotiations as
problem-solving sessions in which you investigate the
problems and then come up with creative solutions
together. Removing the emotional weight from your discussion is the first step. Agree to love one another, no
matter what, and discuss within the context of belonging, not as adversaries. After you have removed the
emotional threat, add the element of togetherness: you
will solve your couple problem together. Expect to put
mutual effort into the solutions you come up with, and
look at it as an opportunity for deeper intimacy.

The basic principles of problem-solving should be
followed in your discussions. First, define the problem
clearly, taking input from both and coming up with a
description of the problem in which both can concur.
List possible solutions in a "brainstorming" session
where you bring forth ideas and refrain from shooting
them down. Be creative; be flexible. Later, you can ana-

lyze the suggestions and agree on the alternative which seems best. If both spouses have different suggestions, strike a compromise solution. When you have come to an agreement, write down your solution — the result of your negotiations — as specifically as possible, including the behaviors which will be required of each partner.

You will also need to tolerate the situation while you work to bring about the desired improvements in your relationship. It is a matter of accepting short-term dissatisfaction to attain long-term goals and rewards. One thing can help immeasurably: to demonstrate consideration, tact, and good manners.

A survey of four hundred counselors has reported *lack of consideration* as the chief cause of marital incompatibility. We also find that bad manners are often a primary source of marriage problems. In marked contrast, treating one another tactfully with careful thought given to the other's feelings will go far to carry you through periods of conflict.

Tact has been defined as the way in which we verbally handle and touch others so that they feel a sense of worth and security. It is, after all, "a kind of mind-reading," Sarah Orne Jewett says. But we lose the ability to do this when we are preoccupied with other things. When personal wishes, distractions, or exhaustion take over, we lose touch with our partner's feelings. Thus, it is better to save discussions for special times when neither is tired and both are free to concentrate on one another. In the meantime, even in the heat of stress, remember that tact plus thoughtfulness equals the consideration your marriage needs.

Understanding and resolving your conflicts will

always require consistent, patient effort and a great commitment of emotional energy. This is the work of marriage which catches couples by surprise. As one wife said, "Who would think we could find that many things to argue about in the course of the first year? We had to work through every detail of our life, from when to go to bed at night to which family to spend Fourth of July with. We even had our disputes about how to rinse dishes and which personal possessions we were willing to share. But we've learned how to adjust to each other — to negotiate and accommodate, and to change when change is needed. Now we're a couple, not just individualists trying to live together. We've made it! At least, we're ready for the next test."

> Commit yourselves to resolving conflicts in ways that bring you closer and forge a stronger partnership. This is the thirteenth step in building a marriage that can survive any difficulties.

SUGGESTIONS

1. Open a new section in your notebook entitled "Conflicts." Record major conflicts in your marriage and how you have resolved them. Go through the steps you took, and compare them with the suggestions in this chapter.

2. Observe your secret choices as you relate to your partner during periods of conflict. Do they help or do they spark fresh turmoil? Make some written commitments concerning more constructive behavior which you intend to put into practice.

3. Study the communication techniques in chapter 5 of our book *The First Years of Forever*.

4. How would you rate your tact/consideration/good manners quotient? Note three times recently when you have been less than tactful or thoughtful with your mate. See what you can learn from the timing and circumstance of these happenings to avoid this behavior in the future.

8

POWER STRUGGLES:
THE SECRET WAR

> Have we learned to respect, adapt, and compromise,
> or are we locked in a power struggle,
> both trying to take control?

What causes fights and quarrels among you? Don't they come from your desires that battle within you? You want something but don't get it . . . (James 4:1 – 2).

Have you considered the possibility that when you're fighting about money, sex, personal habits, child rearing, or in-laws, that's not what you are fighting about? The real issue may be *control,* with the answers to these questions at stake: Who's in control in this marriage? Which one of us has the power to tell the other what to do and when? Which one of us gets his or her own way? Whose rights take precedence? Of course, these questions are seldom verbalized, but they remain the issue.

For instance, counselors and researchers agree that in today's culture, money causes more marital difficulties than almost anything else. They also say that money is not the real problem. It is only a symbol, the sign of power and self-worth. Because the myth that money power buys happiness has been widely accepted, the use of it triggers explosive disagreements. After all, most people today feel entitled to happiness, and those who believe the myth are threatened if money is not available to attain it. The battle over personal habits, also a leading cause of marital discord, boils down to the individual's right to be him or herself and behave accordingly — or the partner's right to demand change. Again, a contest for power. Power struggles are the most common conflict of marriage. They are also the least understood. Think of them as a secret, mostly silent war fought with diversionary tactics, amid confusion as to who the enemy really is. They agitate quarrel after quarrel over matters that are beside the point, and, ultimately, they can destroy your partnership.

Consider these examples of control and the struggle for it, as taken from life in a one-week period.

Couple A fight over who controls the money. He demands that she prove her commitment to their marriage by getting a full-time job. He will handle her paycheck and give her a weekly allowance.

Couple B fight over his right to free time. Although he works two jobs, she tries to control how he spends the rest of his waking hours. "You can't go fishing tonight; remember, it's your turn to clean the bathrooms."

Couple C fight over his enjoyment of wine with his dinner. A new Christian, she tells him, "I will not tolerate social drinking in my house."

Couple D fight over the way he dresses. She: "That shirt and tie look terrible together. And why are you wearing *that* suit?" He: "I don't tell you how to dress. So don't tell me. You're always trying to change me."

Couple E fight over *everything* — sex, dealings with their children, decisions concerning the upkeep of their house, where and when to vacation, the kind of car to buy — the list of controversies in their home is endless. (The first hour of cleaning the garage together can result in World War III.) Neither is in control, neither trusts the other, and both are miserable.

Couple F never fight. She fulfills his expectations to be all things to him when she gets home from a demanding job — to cook the meals he likes, to listen to him, and to be absorbed in him, even though she longs to have time to herself after the pressures of the day. She also runs his errands on her lunch hour, does all the tasks he finds disagreeable, and somehow keeps life moving smoothly for him. She is desperately tired and unhappy.

The secret war depicted in these examples defeats all parties involved, but may give a false sense of victory to one. The tactics employed during power struggles range from nagging, withholding sexual favors, pouting, or totally withdrawing, to threats, yelling, even hitting, and other disagreeable behavior, such as trying to gain control by exposing the partner's weaknesses in front of others. Battering one another with cruel, abusive words is a method frequently used. Bickering becomes the daily diet of many a couple who have not resolved the basic issue of control.

Because each ongoing power struggle is as unique

as the two individuals engaged in it, it is difficult to make predictions as to the outcome. There are several possibilities. The war may continue, bitterly unresolved. One partner may gain the upper hand with the other partner unable to resist. Both may react in passive-aggressive ways with no one at the helm. The couple may fall into the miserable habit of feuding as a way of life. "Partners" may become disgruntled individuals residing in one house but going their separate ways, their marriage existing on paper only. Divorce may be their "final solution." Civil war, dictatorship, anarchy, perpetual unrest, or the annihilation of the marriage are disagreeable choices, indeed.

Ready for the good news? It doesn't have to be like that. Remember the God-given power of your will, not bestowed so that you can trample your mate and obtain your own way, but so that you can make positive choices which will ensure the blessings of marriage for yourself and your partner. By understanding the cause of power struggles and applying biblical solutions, you can eradicate them from your relationship. Only the ordinary differences will remain, to be worked out with courtesy, compassion, and grace. Is that promising too much? It will depend on your response to biblical counsel.

To understand the cause of power struggles we need to return to the Garden where the first man and woman began their marriage under ideal conditions. God intended husband and wife to be a spiritual, functional unity, centered in Him, and living and loving without sin. The marriage ordinance given in Genesis 2:21 – 25 made no provisions for headship, for the first couple began their marriage in joyous unity with perfect order in their relationship. But when sin entered into the world through Eve's deception and Adam's deliberate disobedience, it changed everything.

The couple became *self*-centered and ill at ease, not only with God, but with one another. Their symptoms of mistrust and alienation took root and sprang up like giant weeds in the fertile soil of humankind's newly-acquired sinful nature, with the capacity to choke out love and mar or destroy marriages from that time forth.

Since then we have seen, historically and personally, that the working of sin produces disorder, disintegration, and chaos. And yet we find a greater power at work: God, desiring to restore order and blessing to our lives, if we choose to follow His plan in faith and obedience.

Threaded throughout the Bible is the motif of blessings and cursings. We find this motif imprinted upon marriage, as well as other aspects of life. The verb "to bless" (the great benediction word of the Bible) basically means "to enrich." God is always the source of our enrichment and blessing. "To curse" means "to impose a ban or a barrier, a paralysis on movement or other capabilities." Thus, marriage was designed to enrich our lives, but when sin takes charge, it literally paralyzes the love relationship. The marriage can go nowhere, and the power struggles between husband and wife form what appears to be an insurmountable barrier to blessing.

We know that sin lies at the root of these struggles, but the specific problem is selfishness in its many forms. James explains,

> For wherever there is jealousy (envy) and con-
> tention (rivalry and selfish ambition) there will also
> be confusion (unrest, disharmony, rebellion) and all
> sorts of evil . . . practices (James 3:16 AMPLIFIED).

Selfishness has three children — ugly offspring
named Lust, Pride, and Fear. These are the three forces
which produce the power struggles of marriage, and,
indeed, all power struggles. In every case, the problem
can be traced back to one of the Gruesome Threesome
running amok in human affairs. These three prefer to
go by other names which suggest that right is on their
side. My Rights, My Needs, What's Best for Me, My
Position, I Deserve, and I Am Important are just a few
of their aliases, but the New Testament writers dispose
of all their pretensions.

John says,

> For all that is in the world, the lust of the flesh, and
> the lust of the eyes, and the pride of life, is not of
> the Father, but is of the world (1 John 2:16 KJV).

James concurs,

> What causes fights and quarrels among you?
> Don't they come from your desires that battle
> within you? You want something but don't get it
> (James 4:1 – 2).

It is our lust for *what we want* — for pleasures, for
possessions, and for our own way about things —
which motivates us to quarrel. In a marital partnership,
colliding lusts will inevitably produce power struggles.

So will a situation where one partner thwarts the other's efforts to obtain what he or she wants.

Pride also produces power struggles. Philosopher Ralph Waldo Emerson asserts that "Life is a search after power." The desire to dominate, to prove one's own power and authority, and to authenticate one's sense of self-righteousness, by some form of force if necessary, is as old as Cain.

Finally, there is fear which manifests itself in many forms. We may fear being controlled — losing our self-hood under the domination of a partner. We fear our own weakness and suspect that, unless we fight, we'll be cheated out of our rights. We sometimes fear change and thus fight it all the way, thinking that if we can keep control, we can stop change from happening. Most often, we fear not being in control of our situation; the more fearful we are, the more control we want to exert. In fact, control literally means a counter-roll against the roll or list of a ship. When we fear the ship of our life is rolling too far in one direction, we try to exert control over our partner to correct the situation. Our partner may over-react to compensate for the imbalance in the other direction, and so on. Power struggles!

A key fact to remember about fear is that it is incompatible with love. When fear takes over, there is no place for love. The two cannot stay in the same room (or heart) for long. Which will you choose? John explains,

> There is no fear in love; but perfect love casteth out fear: because fear hath torment. He that feareth is not made perfect in love (1 John 4:18 KJV).

Lust. Pride. Fear. Under this broad outline each of us can fill in the details of our own struggles. Remember that it always takes two for a power conflict. Neither mate is exempt from responsibility.

If we choose, we can look in the Bible as in a mirror to see ourselves the way we really are. As the saying goes, it's not a pretty sight! But always the Bible moves quickly to solutions which can heal, restore, and transform the human condition. In the remainder of the chapter, we want to concentrate on the biblical cure for power struggles, focusing on the epistle of James, which points us to the kind of behavior and perspective which can end the secret war.

Does James understand the conflicts of marriage? You bet! We have only to read his description of the tongue at work:

> We all make mistakes in all kinds of ways, but the man who can claim that he never says the wrong thing can consider himself perfect, for if he can control his tongue he can control every other part of his personality! The human tongue is physically small, but what tremendous effects it can boast of! A whole forest can be set ablaze by a tiny spark of fire, and the tongue is as dangerous as any fire, with vast potentialities for evil. It can poison the whole body; it can make the whole of life ablazing.
> No one can tame the human tongue. It is an evil always liable to break out, and the poison it spreads is deadly. We use the tongue to bless our Father, God, and we use the same tongue to curse our fellowmen, who are all created in

God's likeness. Blessing and curses come out of
the same mouth — surely, my brothers, this is
the sort of thing that never ought to happen!
(James 3:2, 5 – 6, 8 – 10 Phillips).

What's the solution? Wisdom, James says. *True
wisdom.* Wisdom *from above* in contrast to the wisdom
produced by this world and our own lower nature
guided by the Devil. True wisdom from above gives us
the kind of behavior and perspective which can end the
war. How do we know it when we see it? Its first characteristic is humility.

Are there some wise and understanding men
among you? Then your lives will be an example
of the humility that is born of true wisdom. But if
your heart is full of rivalry and jealousy, then do
not boast of your wisdom — and don't deny the
truth . . . you may acquire a certain wisdom, but it
does not come from God — it comes from this
world, from your own lower nature, even from
the devil. For wherever you find jealousy and
rivalry you also find disharmony and all other
kinds of evil. The wisdom that comes from God is
first utterly pure, then peace-loving, gentle,
approachable, full of tolerant thoughts and kindly
actions, with no breath of favoritism or hint of
hypocrisy. And the wise are peacemakers who go
on quietly sowing for a harvest of righteousness
(James 3:13 – 18 Phillips).

Let's take a closer look at this wisdom "from
above" (called "skillful and godly wisdom" in Proverbs

24:3 AMPLIFIED) to determine what it is and how one obtains it. At the core of the New Testament we discover that Jesus Christ, the Son of God and Lord of Life, "has become for us wisdom from God" (1 Cor. 1:30). Through Him we gain an understanding of the true nature of things, and this becomes the basis for the way we live and think. As we recognize who God is, and as we enter into a vital relationship with Jesus Christ, we develop a clarity of insight which makes it possible to understand more and more from the divine perspective. And that is godly wisdom: "the ability to see things from God's viewpoint."

Is this some mystical knowledge which comes in mysterious ways? Not at all. We have been given the Bible in order to learn God's will on almost every issue of life. While not all our questions are answered, we have all of the principles we need to conduct our lives wisely. "Skillful" wisdom comes to us as we spend time reading and studying the Bible on a consistent basis, and putting what we learn into practice. This is how to develop the practical wisdom and mental good sense needed to live life in all areas — including the important area of choices.

The epistle of James reminds us that wisdom also comes from God in response to our asking,

> If any of you lacks wisdom, he should ask God,
> who gives generously to all without finding fault,
> and it will be given to him (James 1:5).

No one should think, however, that God offers instant wisdom on demand, like a heavenly Coke machine. When James speaks of the wisdom that is from above, he uses a present tense participle: "Wisdom *is coming* from above." In other words, we don't get a chunk from the commissary to last us a lifetime, and we don't purchase it on the installment plan. Wisdom comes to us in a steady flow from the mind of God and keeps on coming to meet the demands of our lives, from hour to hour. The supply never runs out, and it is always available to us as we walk with Him in the light of His Word.

Not only does God's wisdom enable us to see rightly and truly from the divine perspective, it also makes it possible for us to behave in wonderfully constructive ways. James describes seven expressions of wisdom in the lives of those who receive it from the Lord moment by moment. This wisdom is:

1. undefiled by our lower nature.
2. peace-loving, rather than combative and contentious.
3. considerate, courteous and gentle.
4. submissive, respectful, willing to yield to reason.
5. full of compassion and good actions.
6. wholehearted, free from doubts and waverings.
7. straightforward, sincere, and not manipulative.

What would happen in your marriage if one or both of you began living out these seven expressions of wisdom? First and foremost, the heat of controversy and bad feelings would be dispelled. Obviously, you can gain much more cooperation from your spouse with this kind of behavior than with threats and acts of war. Therapists warn couples to provide positive reinforcement to one another. Can you think of anything more positive than these expressions of wisdom lived out in your marriage?

Note that wisdom does not close the door to discussions of issues which will inevitably arise in a marital partnership. It does direct those discussions in channels of straightforward, non-manipulative courtesy and sweet reason. You see, wisdom also knows how to communicate. In a few words James shows us the essence of good communication in marriage: "Everyone should be quick to listen, slow to speak and slow to become angry" (James 1:19). The couples who begin listening to one another, controlling their tongues and refusing to take offense are well on the way to moving from war into a state of negotiated peace.

When the heat is off and the bad feelings dispelled, what remains are ordinary conflicts to be resolved by the techniques given in chapter 7. And now, once the issue of power struggles and control has been cooled, you are set free to see all things differently. Wisdom includes both a godly perspective and godly behavior.

For example, in the case of Couple D, the issue of what clothes he wears may no longer be symbolic of the issue of control. She will learn to express herself tactfully, and he will feel free to accept her advice. In fact, he may be pleased that she loves him enough to advise him on his appearance. Now that the war has ceased, he can appreciate her good taste and her valuable assistance.

Similarly, when a husband asks his wife to keep her hair long, she may resent it as an attempt at control.

When wisdom sweetens their relationship, she may be flattered by the delight he has in her long hair, and glad to please him by wearing it that way. It's all in the perspective, and the perspective can be changed by wise behavior.

We need to remember that because we have a sinful nature, pride, fear, and the lust to have our own way will always be controlling factors when the Lord is not in control of our lives and our choices.

James shows us how to turn the control over to the Lord in three important steps.

1. *Submit yourselves, then, to God (James 4:7).*

He reminds us of a basic principle: God opposes the proud but gives grace to the humble. The word for "opposes" is a military term: He *battles* against the proud. As long as we arrogantly fight against Him, we are conducting a losing battle. But if we humble ourselves before the Lord, "He will lift us up" (James 4:10). Anyone who has been lifted up by the Lord knows what a wonderful, life-transforming experience that is. The price we must pay for it is agreement with God about our own foolishness and sinful behavior, and the desire to exchange our lack of wisdom for His grace and love to be poured through our lives.

Lest we forget, He warns us again about arrogant, self-assertive behavior:

> Now listen, you who say, "Today or tomorrow we will go to this or that city, spend a year there, carry on business and make money." Why, you do not even know what will happen tomorrow. What is your life? You are a mist that appears for a little

while and then vanishes. Instead, you ought to say, "If it is the Lord's will, we will live and do this or that." As it is, you boast and brag. All such boasting is evil (James 4:13 – 16).

Since our lives are no more than a puff of smoke, we have no grounds for our arrogant assertiveness in marriage. These are the biblical facts:

1. We don't even know what is going to happen tomorrow.
2. His will, not ours, will be accomplished.
3. Our life is no more than a mist which vanishes away.

When we come to see that our plans are not our own, our time is not our own, and our lives do not even belong to us, we will develop a true perspective of life in which there is no room for self-assertion, but a dependency on God's will. This dependence can bring peace to our hearts and to our marriage.

James also directs us to the principle of taking our needs to God in prayer, rather than trusting power plays and negative approaches to gain our own way with our partner. But the motive of our hearts must be good:

When you ask, you do not receive, because you ask with wrong motives, that you may spend what you get on your pleasures (James 4:3).

The Greek word for "spend" actually meant *squander:* God knows that when we get what we think we want, we're apt to throw it away, like the Prodigal Son who went to a far country and squandered his inheritance before returning to his father. God wants us to pray for every need in our marriage — to pray together, with no ill feeling between us hindering our prayers. He always delights to meet our genuine needs.

Submitting to God also involves submitting to one another. One of the attributes of wisdom, as described by James, is a submissive, respectful, willing-to-yield-to-reason attitude. We are instructed to "be subject to one another out of reverence for Christ" (Eph. 5:21 AMPLIFIED), and the next verses in Ephesians 5 and 6 deal with the order and stability of the home — wives being subject to their husband's loving and protective leadership, and children obeying their parents. In a good marriage, unmarred by power struggles, clearly defined boundaries exist. Everyone knows what is expected of husband and wife; of parents and children.

Such balance does not signify a rigid establishment — a pecking order — but a stable arrangement for relationships and interaction in the home which allows room for variations as needed and mutually agreed upon. The husband and wife are equal partners before God with different roles and responsibilities, and they must be free to work together and interact for constructive change. (In marriages where one is afraid to talk to the other, nothing can change.) Think of compromise as a promise to work things out, a flexible and reasonable approach to the issues to be decided. When our compromise is based on a realistic attitude and a godly perspective it will work!

Within God's order are varied ways of setting up the details of the marriage partnership, sharing responsibility and control according to biblical guidelines and the gifts and preferences of each partner. Marriage partners must achieve a fine balance between dependence and support, with a fair division of the household/family responsibilities, for if both partners are present and in reasonably good health, one partner should not have to bear the burden of the other person or of the family and home all of the time. Partners are to be *helpers*, aiding and supporting one another as friends and allies. (See Gen. 2:18 – 22.)

When we submit to God, we gain the capacity to submit graciously to one another. When we go to God, freely confessing our sins, we receive the ability and desire to go to our mate, confessing where there has been offense; forgiving, and being forgiven. At this point, real healing begins.

2. Resist the devil, and he will flee from you (James 4:7).

God wants us to recognize the real enemy: the Devil himself. Our mate is not our enemy. We have only one real adversary, and he is the enemy of our souls, the enemy of our marriage, the one who is anti-love, who works to bring about divisions, disintegration, and chaos in human affairs.

After we recognize the enemy, we need to know this powerful fact: If we resist him, he will have to flee from us. But if we accept his subtle promptings without resistance, we will slip into evil-doing as naturally as a fish sliding into a stream. According to James, we must exert ourselves to:

> (1) submit ourselves to God's control
>   and authority.

(2) learn from the Bible what good we ought
   to do.
(3) do it! (See James 4:17.)

3. *Come near to God and he will come near to you* (James 4:8).
     Responding to this gracious invitation is the third
step in turning the control of our lives and our marriages over to a loving God. When we do this, control
problems seem to melt away. We still have problems,
challenges, decisions, and the difficulties of life before
us. We still will have to learn to adjust, adapt, and compromise in the details of our partnership. But the fierce
war for control because of our out-of-control fears,
pride, and lusts is settled. We can be moved out of this
place of established peace *only by our own choice.*

> Turn the control of your life and the power
> struggles of your marriage over to God to settle
> the war once and for all. This is the fourteenth
> step in forming a marriage filled with peace.

SUGGESTIONS

     1. In the "conflict" section of your notebook, add
your observations on power struggles in your marriage.
Do they exist? To what extent? Think of issues which
produce fights and quarrels because they represent *control* in your marriage. What area do you most want to
control? Why?
     2. Which one of these phrases best describes your
marriage at this time: civil war, dictatorship, anarchy,
feuding, armed truce, state of negotiations, or established peace? Work on your desired goal and come

back to the question to answer it again, one month from now.

3. How can you implement the biblical plan outlined in this chapter? If you are already in the process of doing so, at what point are you?

4. Read the seven expressions of wisdom at least once a day and ask God to display them in your life. Keep a daily record of how He answers this prayer.

5. Take one small issue which has bothered you from time to time and attempt to resolve it by a combination of compromise, respect, and adaptation.

9

CONFUSION OR ORDER: A MASTER PLAN

> Do we manage our life together in an orderly way according to a master plan, or do we live in confusion, without plan, purpose, or vision of what is most important to us?

For He . . . is not a God of confusion and disorder but of peace and order (1 Cor. 14:33 AMPLIFIED).

Marriage has been described as a continuing exercise in problem solving. Here's another way to look at it: Marriage is an unending parade of decisions demanding your attention — decisions complicated by the fact that two people are sharing one life.

Many of these decisions are major ones which should never be dealt with piecemeal: What sort of life-style do we really want? How should we spend our time and energy? How should we handle our money and what do we want to accomplish with it? How many children should we have and how should we raise them? What about our career goals and plans for further education? How can we nurture our relationship? What kind of environment do we need? What church will we attend? Who will we choose for friends? How do we balance the demands of our respective families on the holidays? How should we allocate responsibility for housework, yard work, paper work, phone calls, grocery shopping, and errands — all necessary in operating our new household? And so on, moving into the less crucial, but necessary decisions connected with establishing your working relationship as lifetime partners.

At the bottom line is a compelling question which must be answered before you can make clear, constructive, and consistent decisions on the other issues. The question: *What is **most** important in our life?*

Have you asked yourselves that question? Do you know the answer? (There may be two answers; it takes some time to become *one*.) When you have agreed on your priorities (whatever soul-searching and debating it takes to come to that point), many of the pressing questions listed above will be resolved, with only the details to be filled in as the need arises.

In other words, your marriage needs a Master Plan, based on your priorities and reflecting what is most important to you, which can guide you in making the decisions which will shape your new life together.

This Master Plan will need to be kept up to date. Some couples schedule an annual or semi-annual "retreat" away from home in a relaxed, secluded setting to re-evaluate their Master Plan, determine how well it's working out in daily life, and set goals for the next year. This also serves as an important "touching base" time for deeper communication concerning their relationship and their individual needs. All sorts of issues can be addressed in a loving, non-judgmental atmosphere with the attitude that this is the time set aside to discover better ways to relate to one another, because it's so important to both of you. It can also be a good time to plan improved ways of running your home or organizing your financial papers. Many useful books are being written on the subject of organizing one's home, possessions, finances, and life in general. You may want to study some of these ahead of time to get new ideas for your planning retreat.

Having a Master Plan and setting aside private times for updating it will eliminate the danger of following two sets of individual dreams which inevitably collide. The Master Plan has room for your dreams as well as goals, but they should be shared, understood, and turned into prayers by both partners. You can, at least, agree to pray, "Lord, if this dream is not in Your plan for our life, please take it out of (his, her, or our) heart. And if the desire is from You, show us how to delight ourselves in You so that You can fulfill the desires of our heart."

The alternative to having a plan is to have none. Couples who muddle through life without a plan face a maze of decisions, large and small, which must be anguished over, one at a time. Then they have to live with the problems which result from indecisiveness or from decisions made haphazardly. Ongoing conflicts and confusion can be expected as the two yoked together pull in different directions.

Your Master Plan should reflect (1) your priorities, (2) your specific goals, and (3) the strategies you want to incorporate to achieve those goals. But, ideally, it begins with *vision*.

What is vision? It's mental sight: the capacity to see what has not yet come to pass, but has potential fulfillment. It is unusual foresight which looks beyond the ordinary and unifies our thinking and planning and expectations. Vision should not be confused with ordinary daydreams. A daydream is a wish made with no real hope of fulfillment, unsubstantial as a cloud. By contrast, vision is forward-thrusting and strong, with power to shape your goals, integrate your marriage, and bring order into your home and your life.

Vision in the Scriptures describes a prophet's revelation from God, but in Proverbs 29:18 it also signifies the entire truth of God's revealed Word: *Where there is no vision, the people perish.* The meaning is plain: Without God's Word, people abandon themselves to their own sinful ways and suffer the consequences. On the other hand, the person who follows God's Word will be "blessed, happy, fortunate, and to be enviable" (Proverbs 29:18 AMPLIFIED).

We often apply this warning to our nation, but how about our marriage? Our home? Our family unit? If we have no vision, no consistent standards or guidance from the Bible, God's revealed truth, what will happen to us? The answer can be found in the word *perish.* The people perish without vision. The picture of perishing that comes to mind is dying in a storm at sea. But the Hebrew word for perish means "run wild, casting off all restraints. Letting your hair down literally or figuratively and becoming disheveled." Related to it are the ideas of becoming loosened, exposed, broken loose and out of control.

As counselors we see families in this kind of upheaval and marriages torn apart by the effects of "perishing" because they had no vision of truth to shape and direct their lives. Without this vision to bind everything together and to give purpose, meaning, and order to the way we conduct our affairs, sooner or later the loose ends of our tangled lives will begin to fray. Unless order takes over, they are apt to unravel completely.

In the New Testament, when God's Word addresses our tendency to anxiety, something like this unraveling is pictured. If you know any Bible verses by memory, you probably have learned this one: "Casting all your cares upon Him, for He careth for you" (1 Peter 5:7). The word for "cares" or "anxiety" is a Greek word which has the idea of *drawing in different directions*. The Scripture says that we need not be pulled this way and that by distracting anxieties because He cares for us *with forethought and interest*. Think of what it will mean to you to make this truth a part of the vision which integrates your life and keeps it together. The vision we're talking about is not only the truth as revealed by God in the Scriptures, but your personal application of that truth to your lives — in other words, the way you live it out.

Your vision for your marriage will not be exactly like any other couple's, but it can be according to God's exciting and specific plan for you, based on scriptural truth. We urge you to share your vision. Put it down on paper in a purpose statement to which you can both agree. After you have clarified your purpose, keep referring back to it; remind each other of it, or it may dissipate. You have a shared life. So wait on God together to discover the unique things He wants you to do with your shared life. Then do what He shows you, and keep the vision fresh.

If your vision is shaped by your commitment to God's truth, it will not only provide the groundwork for a Master Plan; it can lead to finding *the Master's Plan* for you.

Share your vision and work out a Master Plan for your partnership. This is the fifteenth step in building a marriage that succeeds.

OUR SHARED VISION
What Is Most Important in Our Life

_____

_____

_____

_____

_____

_____

Our Purpose Statement for Our Shared Life

_____

_____

_____

_____

Signed _____and_____

Date _____ Place _____

Bible Promise or Instruction _____

_____

_____

Our Priorities

1. _____
2. _____
3. _____
4. _____
5. _____
6. _____
7. _____

Dreams to Pray About

_____
_____
_____
_____
_____
_____

Long-Range Goals

1. _____
2. _____
3. _____
4. _____
5. _____
6. _____

Specific Goals This Year

1. _____

2. _____

3. _____

4. _____

5. _____

Strategies for Accomplishing Our Goals

1. _____

_____

_____

2. _____

_____

_____

3. _____

_____

_____

4. _____

_____

_____

5. _____

_____

_____

Insights on Long-Term Goals and Dreams

_____

_____

_____

_____

_____

_____

Master Plan Retreat

To be held where: _____

To be held when: _____

Evaluation and Update of Master Plan

Priority Changes? _____

_____

_____

_____

Long-Term Goal Changes? _____

_____

_____

_____

How Well Did We Do in Achieving Short-Term Goals?

_____

_____

_____

Strategy Improvements _____

_____

_____

_____

New Short-Term Goals? _____

_____

_____

_____

Bible Verses—Promises, Instructions, Insight _____

_____

_____

_____

Signed _____

10
STRATEGIES FOR YOUR MASTER PLAN

Have we developed any strategies for achieving our goals in marriage?

Authors' Note: Dr. Dow Pursley, a counselor at the Wheat Clinic, spends much of his time working with married couples who are taking positive steps to grow in their relationship. We have invited him to share some of his good ideas.

by Dow Pursley, Ed.D.

Good sex, good communication, good jobs, good school performance, and good marriages all have one thing in common: good preparation and planning. The sad truth is that although most people plan their education and jobs, they do the minimal planning for the relationship that they should be involved in for the rest of their lives: marriage.

Desiring a good marriage is noble, but unless a couple sets goals and develops a good plan to reach those goals, their marriage is only a potential waiting to be actualized! The following strategies are designed to help you plan for and achieve the goals you've set for your marriage.

STRATEGIES FOR MARRIED COUPLES

Spiritual Life Planning

Developing a spiritual plan together is essential. My wife, Joanne, and I went to Dr. Tim LaHaye for pre-marital counseling. He gave us many things to think about, but he strongly suggested three things which I've never forgotten:

1. Pray for each other in the presence of the other every day, calling down God's blessing and favor on each other.

2. Move one thousand miles away from each set of parents for at least the first year of marriage.

3. Telephone Dr. LaHaye, wherever he might be, before taking the step of separating under duress, even for one night.

The idea of praying for each other daily is a good practice for several reasons. Praying with our mate shows that we both are depending upon God for the outcome of our life together. Dr. Wheat says, "It's a time of shared vulnerability before God." Praying and reading the Scriptures together strengthen the marriage bond and make it less vulnerable to the assaults of the world, the flesh, and the Devil.

Successful devotions involve both the husband and the wife and, later, the whole family. Many wives feel that if they initiate devotions, they usurp spiritual authority from their husbands. While it is true that the man is the spiritual leader in the home, I am sure the Lord didn't mean that the wife could never initiate any spiritual activities. Just as the wife often needs help with feeding and dressing the children and other so-called "domestic duties," so the husband can use some help with the spiritual oversight of the home. Only the most insecure man would object to his wife's reminders and offers to help.

Our spiritual plan should also include praying with our children as they come along. This transition from couple praying to family prayer time is much easier if the couple have started out their life together in prayer. I also strongly suggest keeping a family prayer journal, recording the date the prayer was requested, what was prayed for, and finally, the date the prayer was answered. Then highlight the answered prayer in some fluorescent color which will serve later as a reminder to your family of God's faithfulness and goodness.

Sometimes devotions are a problem for couples and families. The start-stop approach is not unusual. If the husband feels pressure that he must always give the devotional, doing all the reading and teaching, he may feel resentful, and the rest of the family may feel bored. However, it can be a source of spiritual growth for parents to watch their children enjoy learning God's principles together, as they take their turn at reading and leading.

In one family I know, family members take turns reading a passage in the Scriptures, and then, starting with the youngest, each asks the child ahead of him or her in age a question about the passage read. This brings out some friendly competition, and the husband tells me that the only problem is that he is the last to answer! Their method is a sure way to keep the college student listening to devotions because the high schooler is bound to ask an obscure and esoteric question.

Many good books are available to help you initiate devotions. I recommend Charles Swindoll's book *Growing Strong in the Seasons of Life* — his book reflects that practical application of biblical truth so needed among our "knowledge-overloaded" Christian generation. Another good tool for elementary school children is *Keys for Kids* (Children's Bible Hour, P.O. Box 1, Grand Rapids, MI 49501). It can be read by the youngest reading child, and is sure to be a big hit with them. (My children have the habit of reading it from cover to cover the day it arrives and still enjoy reading it as a family.)

Take Five (Radio Bible Class, Lincoln, Nebraska) is a short devotional for teenagers which can be read at devotion time. Daily, or at least every other day, the Scriptures should be read along with this.

I think every family should read at least two missionary stories per year — stories about people like George Muller, Hudson Taylor, Elisabeth Elliott, and Amy Carmichael. These will acquaint your children with missions and the stuff great men and women of God are made of. Some other books I suggest your family read are *The Chronicles of Narnia* by C. S. Lewis, *Pilgrim's Progress* by John Bunyan, and *John Foxe's Book of Martyrs*.

It helps to begin small with your devotions, ten to fifteen minutes, and then gradually add new ideas as you think of ways to enhance this time of meditation together. It doesn't have to be done on a daily basis to be effective, but it should be done consistently.

Another area of spiritual life planning has to do with the church. It is important to settle on one church where both husband and wife feel free to worship God. Situations where this simple rule has been ignored can prove troublesome to a new relationship. For example, a couple came in for counseling because they had been married six months and neither wanted to go to the other's church! They finally settled on going to his church Sunday morning and hers Sunday night, reversing the order each week. This lasted several months, and then they tried several churches that neither had attended before. Eventually they found one they both liked and could serve in.

Once you've found a church to attend together, you'll need to plan how many services you will attend each week. Some churches equate faithfulness with church attendance, and people are made to feel guilty if they miss even a mid-week service. Remember that church is not there as an opportunity to impress your pastor or friends, but to facilitate your family's worship of God. Sometimes staying home from a service at night or mid-week provides valuable time for fathers and mothers to spend, both physically and spiritually, with their family.

Communication Strategies

Communication does not come naturally, but talking does! Most of us are good talkers, but few are good at the skill of listening. Genuine communication involves three qualities: "listening, taking the person seriously, and trying to understand."

When any of these qualities are absent, problems in communication result. Beware of failure to listen, lack of eye contact, physical contact, or nonverbal acceptance. Make sure ideas, thoughts, motives, and intentions are clarified. Failure to take the other person seriously (discounting his or her sincerity, feelings, statements, or beliefs) and failure to understand the person's background, emotional state, needs, goals, and desires will close the door to good communication.

Responding is a choice; reacting is a disaster! If we listen, take the person seriously, and try to understand, we can choose to respond in a way that will build the relationship rather than react in a way that will tear it down in a way that will help the other person rather than hurt that person emotionally.

Most hostility results from reacting to the way a person is feeling at any given moment, i.e., angry, upset, or irritated. Remember that ninety percent of communication is *how* something is said (tone, pitch, inflections) and only ten percent involves the content of what is said.

The principle to remember is this: "A soft answer turneth away wrath, but grievous words stir up anger" (Prov. 15:1 KJV). We can, by using this principle, learn to defuse the other's anger by being calm and reassuring him or her of our intentions.

Learning to be a good communicator is important. In marriage, being able to approach each other about what we want, need, and feel is essential, but we need to do it in a Christ-like way which communicates our intentions and helps clarify our motives, thoughts, and actions for our partner.

Beware of communicating the exact opposite of what you truly want. People often do this because they believe they can get the other to change through manipulation. The word *divorce* in marriage is the ultimate manipulator. It invokes fear, anger, depression, rejection, uncertainty, and unreliability. Many people, when confronted with that word, will apologize, try to change, or even make gallant attempts to be different. But manipulation produces no long-term changes, and usually comes back to slap the manipulator in the face.

In the case of one couple, for twelve years the husband regularly threatened his wife with divorce if she didn't change whatever current situation he was complaining about. After years of anxiety, she went to the lawyer and had divorce papers drawn, put them in her top drawer and waited. Sure enough, six months later, he used the magic word again, to which she replied, "Well, I took the liberty of having the papers drawn up the last time you threatened to divorce me, and they are in the top drawer. If you will be kind enough to sign them, this marriage will be history." He was angry, so he signed the papers and their divorce took place.

They saw me later for premarriage counsel before they remarried. Neither had really wanted a divorce. I am convinced that many people who get a divorce never intended to do it; instead, they are attempting to get their mate to change. When it backfires, their pride won't let the process stop.

The only way to see lasting changes develop in anyone is through unconditional love, not manipulation. Unconditional love will evoke lasting change in almost anyone over a period of time.

Financial Planning Strategies

Ninety percent of successful people have written plans and evaluate their plans yearly. The other ten percent are just so smart they don't need to write the plans down!

A spending plan must be agreed upon, and our mates should know the source of our income so they understand where we are financially at all times. The spending plan should include a one-year budget and a seven-year plan. How we give our money, how we save our money, and our accounting of our money all require understanding, compromise, planning, and good verbal communication about long-range goals.

Financial problems are listed in eighty percent of divorces; therefore, having a good plan is not optional, but critical. Most people who come in for counseling have problems in the area of finances, and the most common problem is debt. I always recommend "plastic surgery" on credit cards, and even volunteer my scissors.

More helps for financial planning strategies are found in the following chapter of this book.

Educational Planning

Life is an ongoing educational project for most of us. Teachers need to stay certified, builders need the latest information on their trades, and real estate agents need to upgrade their selling techniques and people skills. As Christians we should plan to be the very best we can be in the calling God has given us. This is part of the creation mandate to subdue the earth.

As a couple, this means we should always encourage our mate to stretch toward excellence. Many couples are so insecure that they see any new challenge taken on by their mates as a threat to their relationship. For example, many women feel a desire to return to college after their children are in school. Sometimes an insecure husband will feel threatened when his wife expresses this desire. One husband told his wife when she said she wanted to attend college, "You are too old." She was twenty-five!

Some insecure wives panic every time their husbands must take a business trip or attend an out-of-town seminar. One woman told me that she gets so depressed when her husband leaves town that she doesn't get out of bed the whole time he is gone. This is a sign of over-dependence and creates great anxiety for the husband.

When a relationship is not growing and healthy, anything becomes a threat to it. But planning for some of these possibilities at the beginning can certainly reduce the anxiety when changes come. We should always encourage our mates to take, or subscribe to, courses, workshops, journals or trade magazines which will help them be more effective in their respective callings.

Self-Esteem Strategies

How we look affects the way we feel about ourselves and how our mates feel about us. I have counseled women with drab clothing, no make-up, their hair arranged in a bun, who were surprised when their husband ran off with a woman who looked just the opposite. There is nothing biblical or spiritual about looking bad. Each person should look his or her best.

Our self-esteem plan should include, when necessary, a diet plan, an exercise program, and attention to our physical appearance, including what we wear and the appearance of our home.

Strategies for Families and In-Laws

Most of us have been taught to honor our father and mother. When they come under verbal attack, we are quick to defend them. If our mate says something unkind about them, it puts us in the unnatural position of choosing between our partner and our parents. Even if our parents have shortcomings (all parents do), we also know their strengths and feel we should point them out to the one doing the criticizing.

I recommend that couples never say anything negative about each other's parents. Always point out the positive. Even if our mate is focusing on negative characteristics in his or her own parents, we must stay positive, or anger toward parents may quickly shift our way.

It is important to decide how often we should visit in-laws and on what basis, including holidays and vacations. It is also important to know what is appropriate to share with our family. As a general rule, we should share as little about our marital difficulties as possible.

Strategies for Relating

Every couple needs a plan which includes dating every week. Here is the dating exercise I recommend.

THE DATING EXERCISE

There are three rules to follow:

1. Alternate choosing the place you think your mate would like to go. It doesn't have to be expensive.
2. Go alone. Do not spend time with friends or relatives.
3. No arguments, not about past issues, current "hot" issues, or potential issues.

Some general guidelines include the following:

1. Treat your mate as you would a first date whom you were trying to impress, and dress for the occasion.
2. The date should include eye contact, physical closeness, and upbuilding conversation.
3. Keep your date out a little longer than you think her parents would appreciate!

THE MARRIAGE CALENDAR

Doing things as a couple or family unites the couple and solidifies their relationship. A marriage calendar enables you to plan weekend activities together or as a family.

I encourage six-month planning with some flexibility. This will allow you to sit down twice a year and plan the weekend activities for the next six-month period. Such planning builds toward the future, solidifies commitment and gives short-range events to look forward to and talk about. Because most couples with children are extremely busy, do not be discouraged if some of the activities are already "planned," but be innovative and build your future together.

The Common Project Exercise

This exercise is designed to help couples re-establish communication over a joint project, perhaps a household task like refinishing furniture, painting a room, planting a garden, or landscaping the yard. Working on a project together builds memories and keeps a couple future-oriented.

The Jar Exercise

Learning our mate's needs is vital. Many couples married for years continue to do things for each other with the intention of giving them pleasure only to find that their mate would have preferred something different, didn't like it at all, or felt that the mate was doing it for himself or herself. This exercise is a good way to learn what your mate really needs.

Find two jars and place them on your respective dressers. On Sunday night place five slips of paper into your mate's jar with one of your needs written on each slip. The needs should be of a personal nature, for example:

1. I need you to hold me fifteen minutes
   before you leave for work this morning.
2. I would like to have thirty minutes
   to relax after I get home tonight before
   I am asked to do anything.

Each day, Monday through Friday, one need is pulled out in the morning and fulfilled before bedtime, so make sure the need can be met in one day. And remember, keep it personal.

Only about five percent of couples who remain together actually grow in their relationship, and this is through their careful planning and conscious effort. Growing a marriage has been likened to growing a garden. Neither happens by accident!

Develop strategies to achieve your goals and carry out your Master Plan. This is the sixteenth step in building an exciting marriage.

11

THE WAY TO FINANCIAL FREEDOM

> Are we free from financial pressures because we
> manage our money, or are we trapped by our
> habit of overspending?

Authors' Note: Because mishandling of money has
become one of the major problems of marriage today,
we offer you the financial counsel from an expert who
will show you how to free yourselves from the debt
trap and avoid the stress of financial worries.

by George Fooshee,
author of *You Can Beat the Money Squeeze*

A few years ago, the Holiday Inn's advertising slogan
was "The best surprise is no surprise." After all the
excitement and glitter of the wedding is over and real
living begins, the best surprise for any young couple is
no financial surprise.

Just prior to celebrating their fifth wedding
anniversary recently, a couple revealed to me some

startling facts about their financial mess. They still owed for their wedding flowers! And the doctor and hospital bill for their first baby was not yet paid.

It has been said that "A panicky present is the result of a planless past." With more than $10,000 in past debts, there is no doubt that the previously mentioned couple has lived in financial panic for their five years of marriage.

FINANCIAL SUMMARY

To eliminate any surprises with money, the couple should fill out a Financial Summary, listing what they own and what they owe. The honest detailing of all resources and obligations will bring about real openness. Completion of this form is an essential first step in facing reality about personal finances, regardless of how long you have been married. You will find that genuine communication about your financial situation will be a tremendous start toward communication in your total marriage relationship. The book of Proverbs confirms the necessity of communication in marriage. "Reliable communication permits progress" (Prov. 13:17 LB).

FINANCIAL SUMMARY
WHERE WE ARE NOW   DATE _____

What we own	Total
Money in the bank, savings	_____
Stocks, Bonds, Investments	_____
Real Estate	
Home (price house would readily sell for on today's market)	_____
Other real estate	_____

Automobiles (current price car
would sell for readily)   _____
Special Property (cameras, guns, hobbies,
motorcycles, silver, camping equipment,
stereo equipment, jewelry, etc.)   _____
Interest in retirement or pension plan   _____

What We Own Totals
Cash & Other Savings   _____
Real Estate   _____
Other Property   _____

GRAND TOTAL OF WHAT WE OWN   _____

	Amount Due	Monthly Payment	Total
To the mortgager of our home	_____	_____	_____
Banks, Loan Companies, Credit Unions, Credit Cards	_____	_____	_____
School Loans	_____	_____	_____
Medical	_____	_____	_____
Other—Family Loans	_____	_____	_____
GRAND TOTAL OF WHAT WE OWE	_____	_____	_____

RECAP
What We **Own** Grand Total   _____
Less What We **Owe** Grand Total   _____
What We Have Accumulated (Net Worth)   _____

Analyze the resources. Do you have surplus items? Are you car rich (two relatively new costly cars) and cash poor (too little cash savings)? Do you have surplus items that could be sold or traded for other items you need? The financial summary will enable you to face the facts about your existing marital finances.

Warning! If what you owe exceeds what you own,

face these facts. You are in hock! You are a debtor! Your
financial past has revealed desires beyond your means.
These figures should be shared with a wise Christian
counselor. If you are an engaged couple, some questions to discuss are: Should our present financial condition change the kind of wedding we have planned? Can
we afford the honeymoon we want?

The Bible says, "The wise man looks ahead. The
fool attempts to fool himself and won't face facts"
(Prov. 14:8 LB).

THE BUDGET

Don't panic and try to avoid doing a budget because
you aren't an accountant or figures aren't your thing.
Two simple definitions of a budget should put you at
ease.

First, a budget is simply *planned spending.* Having a
plan for spending will help build marital harmony and
reach family goals.

A second definition of a budget is *telling your
money where you want it to go rather than wondering
where it went.*

Weekly I talk to couples in all stages of life who
have made a mess of money management, and I see the
trauma, the tears, and the tension resulting from mis-
management. Of the hundreds in trouble, I've asked the
same question: "Do you have a budget? Do you have a
plan for your spending?" None of these couples in
financial distress has ever answered this question with a
"yes."

As a first step to establishing a budget, you should

estimate your living expenses on this Financial Goals form. The categories include the most common expenses.

OUR FINANCIAL GOALS

	Monthly	Annually
1. Tithes & Offerings	_____	_____
2. Federal Income Tax	_____	_____
3. State Income Tax	_____	_____
4. Social Security Tax	_____	_____
5. Other Taxes	_____	_____
6. Shelter	_____	_____
7. Food	_____	_____
8. Clothing	_____	_____
9. Health	_____	_____
10. Education	_____	_____
11. Life Insurance	_____	_____
12. Gifts	_____	_____
13. Transportation	_____	_____
14. Personal Allowances	_____	_____
15. Vacations	_____	_____
16. Savings	_____	_____
17. Household Purchases	_____	_____
18. Debt Reduction	_____	_____
19. _____	_____	_____
20. _____	_____	_____
21. _____	_____	_____
TOTALS	_____	_____
Total Estimated Income	_____	_____
Difference Between Income and Expense	_____	_____

NOTES FOR OUR FINANCIAL GOALS

These explanations of each category will guide you in arriving at the amount for each spending category. Start with the first category and work through them in order. If you have a monthly estimate, multiply it by twelve for the annual figure. If you have an annual figure, divide it by twelve for the monthly figure. Refer to your checkbook to obtain previous expenditures. Don't quit because you can't come up with a figure. Make a guess. The budget process will let you find out how close your guess is.

1. Tithes and offerings: all charitable giving.

2. Federal Income Tax: all amounts withheld, plus estimates paid, plus any amounts due with tax return.

3. State Income Tax: same as above.

4. Social Security Tax: Determine current percent withheld.

5. Other Taxes: any additional tax on your wages.

6. Shelter: a. If renting, include rent, utilities, household supplies, appliance repairs, telephone, other home-related expenses. b. If you own a home, include house payments, insurance, real estate taxes, repairs and maintenance, other items listed under renting.

7. Food: grocery store items, paper goods, cleaning supplies, pet foods, all eating out, carry-out items, and school lunches. May also include entertainment.

8. Clothing: purchases, cleaning, repairs. May be divided with separate budget for each family member.

9. Health: health insurance, medical, dental, hospital expenses, prescriptions, cosmetics.

10. Education: school supplies, lessons, college expenses, uniforms, equipment.

11. Life Insurance: all premiums whether paid monthly, annually, or quarterly.

12. Gifts: birthdays, anniversaries, special occasions, Christmas, weddings, funerals, office collections, dues for organizations.

13. Transportation: gas, oil, repairs, licenses, personal property tax, auto insurance, car payments or an amount set aside to purchase your next car.

14. Personal allowance: for each family member to spend personally, such as hair care, recreation, baby sitting, hobbies, children's allowances.

15. Vacations: Trips, camps, weekend outings, trips for weddings, funerals, family visits.

16. Savings: Amounts set aside now for future needs.

17. Household Purchases: For major appliances, furniture, carpeting, and major home maintenance such as roofing and painting.

18. Debt Reduction: Includes all payments on debt not included in other categories, such as school loans, amount owed to relatives, banks, or on credit cards.

After you've discussed and added the figures, and discussed and added some more, realistically face the total. Can you live within your income? Did you grow tense while talking about money? Angry? Non-communicative? The Bible asks: "Can two walk together unless they be agreed?" (Amos 3:3). Can you be cheerful givers? (If you don't start giving early as a married couple, you will tend to be always stingy toward God.) God loves a cheerful giver.

Are you now saving, "The wise man saves for the future, the foolish man spends whatever he gets" (Prov. 21:20 LB)? Putting off saving while you are young is a real trap. It will never be any easier to save, especially if you procrastinate now. To manage money well, savings must become a habit on paydays, just as giving must be a holy habit.

Warning! If your budget won't work on paper, it won't work period. You may find that your budget won't balance.

Most of us want more than we can afford. So-called "easy payments" and readily available credit cards seem to make it possible for us to spend more than we make . . . for a time.

The average American family has to pay out twenty-three percent of net monthly income just for those "easy payments." For a young couple to achieve this heavy debt position requires only two debt areas — two student loans and one new car payment.

With student loans of $16,000 and a car loan of $8,000, monthly payments can easily be $400 (figuring eight percent for ten years on the $16,000 and fourteen percent for four years on the $8,000).

Most couples will discover that they can't balance their budget with any debt payments at all, let alone $412 a month. What's the solution? GET OUT OF DEBT! Great idea! But how?

By *emergency action!* Sell your new car. Buy an old car for a few hundred dollars that will most likely get you every place you need to go. Move close to work. Use public transportation. Ride a bicycle or moped. Share a car with another couple.

Move into free or very inexpensive housing. Share a home with another couple. Pray for an older couple who will allow you to live in their upstairs, basement, or extra bedrooms in return for lawn mowing, car washing, housecleaning, and other services.The couples I know who have escaped debt in a short time have made temporary short-term sacrifices, usually in the areas of housing and cars — their two largest expenses. By eliminating a $200 to $400 car payment and at least $500 a month for rent and utilities, from $700 to $800 per month is available to pay on the student loan payments. The debt can be paid off in 18 months rather than 120 months!

You may think such action isn't possible. Yet, by prayer and standing on God's promises of provision, thousands of couples annually leave homes and jobs and follow God's leading to attend seminary or graduate schools. Adopting the same kinds of living action that I term "emergency action," they experience His provision.

KEEPING THE BUDGET

Not only do you need to balance your budget, but you also have to keep your budget. Each of your financial goals represents a spending category such as shelter, food, and clothing.

A budget page is similar to a checkbook register, but each page includes only one spending category. For example, visualize a checkbook register that contains only your income and spending for the Shelter Category of your budget.

CATEGORY SHEET

Category **Shelter**　　　　Budget Amount $560.00

Date	Description	Income	Out-Go	Balance
1-1	Deposit from pay	$560.00		$560.00
1-3	Rent		$400.00	160.00
1-5	K-L Electric Co.		52.00	108.00
1-9	Clear Water Co.		12.00	96.00
1-10	Clean Trash Co.		8.00	88.00
1-12	Bell Telephone Co.		12.00	76.00
1-14	Daily News Subscr.		36.00	40.00
2-1	Deposit from pay	$560.00		600.00

This shelter category sheet shows where and how much was spent for housing and gives you a means of monitoring your progress. A total budget is done by having similar pages for each spending category. My wife Marjean and I have kept records for more than thirty-four years of marriage. In addition, we made it a rule never to borrow money to buy anything other than our home.

If only we could sit with you and share how God will bless your decision to live debt-free, even if you have to pay off debt now with *emergency action.* The discipline of your personal finances will encourage discipline in other areas. You will learn to say *no!* to this, in order to say *yes!* to that. The result may well be the abundant life that Jesus promised.

You can experience God's peace and blessing as you learn to plan your giving, saving, and spending. Christ came to set us free. You can achieve freedom from debt depression by carefully and realistically budgeting your wedding and living expenses. Budgeting will ensure that you grow as wise stewards of what God provides.

> Learn how to manage your money to accomplish your goals and to avoid the unhappy consequences of overspending. This is the seventeenth step in establishing a strong marriage.

12

IN-LAWS AND OTHER CHALLENGES

> Are our relationships with our in-laws moving toward loving harmony, growing tensions, or open warfare?

Authors' Note: In-law clashes, stepparenting, age differences, and unexpected career changes will trouble many a marriage in the 1990s. We have asked one wife to share her learning experiences in these areas. We believe that her hard-won victories coming out of seeming defeat testify to God's grace and the importance of one's secret choices more powerfully than anything we could say to you about in-laws and other challenges.

by Victoria James

The title of this chapter implies that in-laws are a challenge — something to be conquered or overcome. I'd rather think of the in-law relationship as an adventure, one not unlike that of building a bridge. Sometimes you feel as if you are trying to cross the Grand Canyon and other times it seems to be just a few stepping stones across a brook. It is an adventure that does, admittedly, present some challenges.

The term *in-law* can immediately conjure up every bad mother-in-law joke you have ever heard and bring visions of your mate's family dissecting you, just hoping to find something wrong. Every insecurity you ever felt suddenly rears its ghastly head because you know that *they* are going to see only the worst in you. Naturally, up goes the defensive wall!

Unfortunately, every segment of the entertainment industry has for years used the in-law relationship, especially the mother-in-law, as negative comic relief. Waiting in grocery store check-out lines, we can leaf through periodicals with headlines like the one emblazoned on the *National Enquirer*: **HOW TO KEEP YOUR IN-LAWS FROM DESTROYING YOUR MARRIAGE.** No wonder we dread, even fear, these terrible people who are going to make our lives miserable. We have been "trained" to see our in-laws as the cross we must bear in order to be married to the one we love. But I, personally, see the in-law relationship as a vital and positive force in marriage. At least, it has been that for me.

Right now you may be thinking, *This gal's in-laws probably adored her from the moment they met, and the worst argument they ever had was over who was going to bring what to the family reunion.* Wrong! My in-law relationship has not been a merry little jaunt down Happiness Lane. It has been more like a roller-coaster ride, running the gamut from loving acceptance to painful rejection. I was, of course, the victim of *in-law persecution* — completely blameless and totally baffled by the disagreements that seemed to keep popping up out of nowhere. (If any of you believe that, I know of a bridge in Brooklyn I'd like to speak to you about.)

Before you decide that I have just confirmed your worst suspicions about in-laws, let's take a look at a different picture. I hope that sharing my own experience with the in-law relationship will give you some insights that can help you build your bridge to a positive, loving, and rewarding relationship with your partner's family. The main components, for me at least, have been understanding, patience, and communication (none of which were my strong points). Although understanding, patience, and communication may seem obvious, there are times, in the stress of the moment, when the obvious becomes obscure and simplicity becomes a complicated jigsaw puzzle.

My first visit to my future in-laws' home was to celebrate my fiancé David's birthday. David didn't think to warn me that his family celebrates birthdays (and all traditional occasions) more formally than I was used to. My first thought when I saw the dining room was, *This is a three-fork family, and I'm a one-fork woman.* At least I hadn't worn my blue jeans and tee shirt!

The next surprise came when we all gathered around the table, held hands, and said grace. At this point, David and I had been dating for three months, but he had never told me that he came from a Christian family. In retrospect, I realize that his Christian character, which made him stand out from the other men I knew, should have been at least a clue. Don't misunderstand. I had trusted Christ as a child when my Grandma took me to Sunday school. But I was not reared in a church-going, grace-saying, Christ-centered home, and, sadly, I had for some time been wandering off course in my walk with the Lord. To be honest, if I'd wandered much further, the Lord would have had to send out a search and rescue team. (On second thought, maybe He did when He brought David and his family into my life.)

At this birthday dinner, I got my first glimpse of one of the most important things that needs to be understood and dealt with in the in-law relationship: diversity of background. In other words, this *ain't* your family, and they may do things differently than you're used to. For me, those differences encompassed broad territory: differences in religious upbringing; different traditions and different ways of celebrating them; the closeness of the extended family unit; and differences in the way problems, especially anger, were handled. This was one of those Grand Canyon times; David's family background seemed about as far removed from mine as you could get.

This is where *had I known then what I know now* comes in. Had I acknowledged and voiced my concerns to David and his family from the beginning, it would have saved us all a lot of heartache and confusion. I failed to begin building that bridge and, instead, started piling up "junk" — resentments, false assumptions, and insecurities — that began creating a wall between my in-laws and me. Ironically, they weren't even my in-laws yet!

They were unaware of the problem because of my failure to communicate. I had even managed to fall into the role of a child with my mother-in-law: she is a very motherly person. It was refreshing to be mothered at the tender age of thirty-one after so many years of being totally responsible for myself and my daughter. It was a nice change of pace to have someone making a fuss over me, and I basked in the glow of attention. It's a shame I didn't have enough sense just to enjoy it.

But my independent nature became contrary when the time came to plan the wedding. Since I had been married before, I wanted a simple, informal, outdoor wedding — very low-profile. My family had long since decided that I could make my own decisions (they weren't going to be able to attend anyway), so I expected to do things the way I wanted. David, however, was the first child in his family to get married, and his family wanted a more traditional, formal affair. Knowing that we were both short of money, they generously offered to pay for flowers, a reception, and even offered their home for the ceremony. Here was another prime opportunity to work on that bridge. A little patience, understanding, and communication would have gone a long way, but, instead, I just kept piling up that "junk."

I grudgingly agreed to suits, ties, dresses, and all the other traditional trappings, but I insisted on an outdoor ceremony. As is usually the case, stubbornness had its price, for our wedding day was windy and chilly. Because it was early spring, my hay fever went crazy and I was miserable. I'd really shown them! Anyway, I reassured myself, I was marrying David, not his family. We could go on from there and build our own little world. We would, of course, include our families in our life, but we would *not* let them dictate to us.

Unfortunately, I was ignoring a few basic facts: (1) Both of you bring your family history, good and bad, into your marriage. (2) You will always have to deal with some sort of in-law relationship. Remember, "in-law" does not stop at mother and father; it extends to brothers, sisters, grandparents, aunts, uncles, and cousins. And (3) "old habits die hard." I had had a tumultuous history in relating to my own parents, and even more difficulty in coping with my former in-laws, so I was prickly about anything that even hinted of parental interference. This led to unnecessary tension with my in-laws, most of which came out of a lack of understanding on both sides.

You see, my lack of communication and failure to be open about my past family relationships gave my in-laws no opportunity to get to know the real me — the person behind that defensive wall I'd built. My self-protective caution prevented me from getting to know my in-laws. As a result, I made a lot of assumptions that just weren't true. Assumptions can be a negative force. I have found since that when I made assumptions about someone else's thoughts or feelings, I was taking the easy way out, for I was afraid to openly confront the problems. It was easier to assume the worst. Today I am very thankful that my in-laws had more patience than I did, or we would probably still be "on the outs."

Our relationship has, at times, been very strained. I was like a keg of dynamite with a short fuse. When I got mad, I was mad all over and very vocal. I lashed out at whoever made me angry and anyone else who happened to be in the line of fire at the time. My in-laws tend to be more analytical and reasonable when dealing with anger. That's not to say they don't speak plainly, but they also listen to the other side. Not me! When I'm mad, there is only one side to be heard — mine.

David's family handled anger so differently! The

problem was that they were *nice* — totally new territory to me. I didn't know how to deal with *nice*. I had grown up learning by example that anger was the way to deal with almost any unpleasant thing. I had been trained to deal with pain, hurt feelings, grief, and other negative emotions with either the "brave little buckaroo" attitude or anger. Anger was the method chosen most often in my family; thus, I found anger the most comfortable approach to handling anything other than "jump in the air" happiness. It was not a good approach, believe me! No one knew how to take my anger, including my husband, and it got pretty lonely over there in my mad corner!

My in-laws must have seen me as some kind of wild woman and wondered how their poor son would ever survive living with such a shrew. But don't give up on me yet. (My husband didn't!) I have come to see that the old patterns in my life were very destructive and have worked heart and soul to develop new patterns. I've learned to confront my true feelings and deal with them appropriately. My husband and my in-laws are aware of the true problem now, and we all work together to deal with the actual emotion (hurt feelings, or in some cases, anger) involved in the disagreements that do inevitably arise in human relationships. This wise saying from Alexander Pope's *Essay on Criticism* has come to mean a lot to me:

> Good nature and good sense must ever join;
> To err is human, to forgive divine.

Anger was not the only thing our families handled differently. In my family, personal grief is just that:

personal. In David's family, it is something to be shared; they have a strong support system and rally around each other to offer comfort and help. I believe that is a healthy, loving attitude, and I feel comfortable with it if the other person needs help. But when I need help, I tend to withdraw into myself, not wanting to "impose" my pain and hurt on others. It took a very painful loss for me to see the error in my thinking and to realize yet another difference in our backgrounds.

I suffered a miscarriage shortly after we had announced that the first grandchild for David's family was on its way. David and I desperately wanted this child. Even though David was an excellent stepparent and loved my daughter, he wanted a child of his own blood. His family was, of course, ecstatic. But when we lost our baby, I wanted to be left alone to suffer our grief and loss. (I didn't know then the old Jewish proverb, *A friend is not a friend until you have cried together*.)

My parents have several grandchildren, and, though they welcome each new addition enthusiastically, they held the attitude, "Something must have been wrong and it is probably for the best. We are glad you are okay. Just go on with your lives and try to forget about it."

In contrast, David's mother and grandmother came to be with me in the hospital and brought me flowers. I would not even see them. I was totally insensitive to David's family and refused to share my grief with them, even though they had suffered the loss of their much-anticipated grandchild. My bridge was getting no attention whatsoever. Not only was I failing to build a bridge to my in-laws; I was destroying the framework that was already there!

As you might have guessed, it all got worse before it got better. My in-law relationship did, in fact, completely deteriorate. It reached a point where, because of a monumental misunderstanding based on false information about a very serious matter, I was disowned by David's family and told I would never be welcome in their home again. The details of this strange episode are not important, but the principle is. It never could have happened if we had kept the lines of communication open. But God used this situation, terrible as it was. Believe it or not, things started turning around.

It was very painful for me to accept the fact that I was never going to be a part of David's family. I didn't realize how much I would miss them and how precious they were to me. If only I had done more bridge building when I could!

I had made so many mistakes. I had expected my in-laws to be the "perfect family" I had always dreamed of. I had put my mother-in-law on a pedestal (a mistake we should never make in any human relationship, for pedestals will inevitably crack and crumble), and then felt betrayed when she fell off. I wanted understanding and total acceptance, but didn't give any. I needed patience and had none; worse yet, I did nothing to develop any. And I had managed to create a rift between my husband and his family. Talk about feeling lower than a snake's belly — I had to look up to see the snake!

But I didn't give up. God graciously helped me to see a flicker of light at the end of the tunnel. I needed to work through that tunnel to climb back to the surface and start building the all-important bridge. I took the first step by calling my father-in-law at his office. (I knew my mother-in-law was too outraged to talk to me just then.) I tried to open the door to some sort of communication, and he advised me to let things be for awhile until everyone had calmed down. Much to my surprise, my mother-in-law called me that very afternoon.

I think we both felt at the time that there was nothing to lose, so we had a frank, open, and painfully honest discussion. It took a heart-wrenching effort on both sides, but we did manage to reach some agreements on developing a better relationship. One of the most important steps for me was removing the titles and beginning to think of my in-laws as people with whom I wanted to build a friendship. To me, certain titles, especially that of *in-law,* carry negative connotations, which I can't yet put aside. This is a personal hang-up and I hope it's not true for you. I surely do get along better with my *friends* than I did my *in-laws,* and we have managed to traverse the Grand Canyon. The little creeks we occasionally encounter are definitely crossable.

In-law problems, like problems in any other relationship, are never one-sided. But the truth is that I *was* stubborn, prideful, and ornery. None of these traits are conducive to good communication, and without continuing, open, and honest communication no relationship will have a solid base.

I don't want to project a completely bleak picture of the last six years. It wasn't all bad. We had happy, fun-filled experiences. We went on a family camping trip, had many joyful family celebrations, and, at my request, my mother-in-law and I had a daily one-on-one Bible study hour during my first year in David's family. Our times of good fellowship around God's Word and her gentle guidance led me back to what I had truly wanted all along — a closer walk with the Lord. I believe God laid the foundation then which made it possible for us to reconcile later at a time when the division between us stretched miles-far and chasm-deep.

My in-law relationships are an important part of my life today, and I know that my husband is much happier when those he loves are in harmony. Thus, the building of the bridge that closed the gap between David's family and me has strengthened our marriage and enriched my life.

One of the most important things I have learned is that you can never have too much love or too many friends. My in-law relationship has been a wonderful source of both. I pray that your adventure in building a happy in-law relationship will be an exciting, positive experience which brings more love and new friendships into your life.

SOME OTHER CHALLENGES

Stepchildren

This is definitely a big-league challenge! May I quote some research results which suggest a less than bright future for the marriage where stepchildren are present.

Two sociology professors from the University of Nebraska, Lynn White and Alan Booth, interviewed more than 1,600 families in 1980 and again in 1983, and found that the most difficult marriages to hold together were second marriages to which both partners brought children from a previous union. White said, "Our evidence indicates that if these couples divorced, *it was because they wanted to get rid of the stepchildren, not the spouse.*" White went on to mention *the striking early divorce pattern* due to the special stress involved in stepparenting. And having a child together to unite the families more strongly didn't help the marriages last either, according to the researchers. (Findings published in *The American Sociological Review*, Vol. 50, No. 5, and reported by *Psychology Today*, June 1986.)

When David and I made our lifetime commitment, I did not know just how difficult it can be to marry a second time with an adolescent child to incorporate into the new family. Ann, my daughter, turned twelve the day after our wedding, and we wanted so much to become a family unit that David and I postponed our honeymoon to celebrate her birthday with her.

Ann and David had related well as long as we were merely dating, and even during our engagement period, but the day we married she suddenly turned hostile, defiant, and just plain difficult. It shocked me, but David took it all in stride and acted as if nothing had changed. He was still kind and loving, even when she was sullen and ornery, but it tore me apart — to be pulled between the two people I loved most in the world. We did our best to reassure Ann that we had no intention of trying to cut her off from her father, and David made it clear that he was not trying to replace her father. We did want to create a solid family base for Ann, something she had never experienced.

David and I had joyfully entered into our marriage with a fairy tale dream of becoming "the perfect family." It was a nice dream, but Ann had her own fairy tale in mind — something along the line of Cinderella without the happy ending. David and his family did everything possible to make Ann feel accepted and loved. She was treated like a princess, and acted like a hag. She resisted all efforts to draw her into her new stepfamily, and I was more than a little upset with my daughter's pigheadedness. My fervent desire for a happy family unit blinded me to the emotional conflict and pain that Ann was going through.

Ann felt, as many stepchildren do, that if she liked David and accepted his family, she would be showing disloyalty to her father and his family. I found it hard to understand the blind loyalty she suddenly developed toward her father. He could do *no* wrong, even when he remarried without telling her and just showed up one weekend with a new wife (and another stepparent for her).

Although David was hurt, he remained steadfast and consistent in his relationship with Ann. Together we have tried to maintain a united parental front, sharing in the decision-making process, but I have not always been as consistent as David. As the natural parent, it was hard for me to let go of my overly protective single-parent attitude and learn to share my parental role with someone who had never been a parent. (The truth was that David could deal with Ann better than I because he could remain objective.) Although I never voiced the "that's my child, not yours" routine, David could sense it in some of my reactions.

David was not the only one sensing my protective attitude. Ann seemed to have a radar system even the

Navy would envy! She could always hone in on the slightest discord and try to plant seeds of discontent and doubt to separate David and me.

Parenting a testy, obstinate adolescent is difficult at best, and beginning a new marriage with a teenager in the house is like trying to mix water and oil. Things like privacy, quiet time together, and little romantic candlelight dinners at home become treasured luxuries.

Ann did everything she could to make her presence felt. Some of her tactics were less than subtle. If David and I were seated on the couch together, she would find a way to wriggle in between us; if we were trying to talk to each other, Ann suddenly needed my immediate help with some problem. In fact, she had a wide assortment of tricks to keep my attention focused on her.

She had reveled in my attention for so many years. Actually, we were too close. I had lost some of my parental authority, and she had become very possessive of me. It was understandable, but frustrating, that she resented having to share me with another person, especially someone she was expected to accept in an authority role. I began to feel like a circus juggler as I tried to divide my time and attention evenly between David and Ann. It was an impossible task: a woman's roles can never be equally divided. I kept hoping Ann would see that David was not taking anything away from her. But in trying to keep everything equally balanced between David and Ann, I was forgetting God's clear plan for marriage: that husband and wife leave all else and cleave together and become one. A child, no matter how deeply loved, can never be a part of that oneness and should not be allowed to compete with it.

I made the mistake of trying to make my husband and child equal priorities when my marriage should have been my first priority. If I had kept my "house" in proper order, we all would have been happier. Ann could not have found those tiny little cracks where she was able to drive a wedge, and David would not have had to suffer the insecurities which those wedges created.

In our case, Ann's natural father actively worked to prevent Ann from getting close to David. He did all that he could to foster her resentment. Nevertheless, for the past six years David has faithfully assumed the responsibilities her natural father cared little about. He has attended school functions, parent/teacher conferences, and every extracurricular activity where she needed support. He has helped her with her schoolwork, acted as a buffer during mother/daughter clashes, and this year he even taught her to drive!

I asked David what he thinks it takes to be a stepparent, and he gave six suggestions which I pass on to those of you who may be in similar situations:

1. Don't try to replace the natural parent.
2. Be consistent and steadfast.
3. Let the child know you are there as a friend.
4. Maintain the authority role, however.
5. Don't try to "win the child over" or buy love.
6. Don't expect thanks or recognition for your efforts.

I realize now that unless a child is very young, the child will probably not be receptive to a stepparent, and it is better to approach the marriage with a realistic acceptance of that fact. After talking to friends and acquaintances who have been either in the stepchild or the stepparent role, I find a general consensus that stepparents are not outwardly accepted or appreciated until the child has been away from home for awhile. But then, do any of us truly appreciate our parents, step or natural, until we are out on our own and using the skills they've taught us?

Yes, stepchildren will be a challenge in almost any marriage, but when two become one in a biblically based marriage, the challenge becomes less intimidating. Actually, there's more love to go around for the children, and they have the benefits of stability and order and security in their home setting. This can only do them good, not harm. They may demand more unconditional love than you ever thought you could give, but God will provide that too.

What a comfort to know that the Lord does guide us through this most prickly area of a second marriage.

Age Differences

When David and I married, he was twenty-three and I was thirty-two, but neither of us considered the fact that I was nine years older a challenge. Unfortunately, some of our friends seemed to think it was a critical area of concern and felt compelled to remind us of it — constantly!

As I look back on it, I wonder if these people were truly concerned about our future together, or if they thought we were just too dumb to do simple arithmetic. The fact was that David knew how old I was all along, and I assumed he was older than he was. He has one of those ageless faces — neither young nor old — and by his own choice he had been working since the age of fourteen and living on his own since the age of eighteen. David was more mature and responsible than any man I had ever dated, and by the time I found out about the age difference, my heart had already made a private but eternal commitment to him.

True love knows no age limits, and I am glad that David and I were unconventional enough not to worry about what other people thought, and to follow our own best judgment on the matter. We did not let our emotions blindly lead us into marriage, for we were both committed to the permanence of marriage and we wanted no mistakes. We spent a lot of time getting to know each other on an intellectual basis; we knew early on that we had connected at the emotional level! We found many common interests and just enough differences to make life interesting. Our age difference did show up in our taste in popular music, but we found a compromise between the Beatles and Three Dog Night — we listened to Alabama instead.

Have there been any "age" problems? I have felt a bit insecure occasionally — after all, he is gorgeous and women are always attracted to him. But he has never wavered in his love, devotion, and total loyalty to me. Our marriage has not always been in perfect harmony (that might be boring), but our discord has rarely been because of the difference in our ages.

I have seen people walk away from what could have been happy relationships because "society's" opinion frightened them. One of my best friends suffered two years of loneliness because she was older than the man she loved. After seeing how happy David and I were together, she finally accepted the younger man in her life when he proposed for the umpteenth time, and they are now happily married.

Today, the trend is changing. More marriages between younger men and older women are taking place — a satisfactory arrangement for both, according to all I have read on the subject. In our case, age played no part in our attraction to one another — we just belonged together and knew it! From our experience, the anticipation of problems connected with age differences can be much worse than any actual problems that may emerge.

When people ask my opinion, I say, "Don't look at the birth certificate; look at the person, his (or her) mind, heart, and soul. You're not going to be cuddling up to a birthdate, but to a person."

Adapting to Career Changes

As a career woman with a secure job in the social work field at the time I married, I valued my independence. Since then I have learned some hard lessons in the process of adapting to my husband's plans.

First, David took a new job which required us to move to another town, and I accepted a position as a bookkeeper. That move wasn't so bad, for, in that city, our Christian foundations were strengthened. (How much I would need that a little later on!)

Two years later, David made the decision to go to college in another state, and so we were off and moving again. As it turned out, Ann hated her new school, I couldn't find a position in my field, and David decided school could wait for awhile. We missed our friends, and as far as I could see, the only good thing that happened there was David finding a job in his profession at higher wages. During this time I nursed an elderly relative through a seven-month illness which proved to be terminal — a traumatic experience — and I myself had to be hospitalized with stress-related symptoms and exhaustion. After a few months of much-needed rest, I found a secretarial position with a salary of less than half of what I had been making before we moved. By now I was convinced that this independent career woman had lost control of her life. I also suspected that God was punishing me for something, but I was soon to know the truth about that.

Just as I was beginning to settle into this new lifestyle, something truly shocking occurred. My husband came home and told me he had decided to join the Army to receive the education he needed to enter a new profession in the mental health field. As if in a bad dream, the wheels of the United States Army began to roll over the secure life I had tried to construct with my husband. David was stationed a thousand miles from home, and after basic training, he was shipped to another base, more than a thousand miles away in the other direction, for Advanced Individual Training. For seven months David and I were separated — we who could never bear to be separated, even for a night.

David's income went from $600 a week to little more than $600 a month, and I took on two extra part-time jobs to keep a roof over our heads while he was away. To say that I was angry, that I felt deserted, would be an understatement.

David's timing could not have been worse, as far as I was concerned. The longer he was away, the more desolate I became. As I grew more tired and more lonely, my coping ability bottomed out. One night I collapsed in bed and began praying from the very depths of my soul. I poured my heart out to the Lord and confessed my weaknesses, and my sins of hard-heartedness, judgmental behavior, and many other sins of the heart. I asked forgiveness and pleaded with God for the strength, patience, and guidance I felt I had lost. I told the Lord that I couldn't make it on my own resources any longer — I needed Him to take control of my life and lead me in His will.

And then I discovered that the Lord had not been punishing me at all, but "child-training" me. He saw me falling back into my old patterns of willful independence and proud self-reliance, and He used this surprising turn in my life to bring me to Him with a heart hungry for His guidance and comfort.

David had already followed the Lord's guidance, and although he was lonely and homesick, he was doing his best to follow that guidance in an honorable way. I am so proud of his strength of character, of the honors he has received, and of the rewarding work he is doing now. I also see how the Lord used my husband's decision (the decision I so bitterly resented) to draw me to Himself. This week David and I will celebrate our sixth wedding anniversary — together again and closer than ever after the pain of our time apart from one another.

What have I learned that could be of help to blended-family couples? That God can — and *will* — use anything in our situations to help us grow up into Christ. This includes the challenges of marriage — whether it be in-laws, or stepchildren, or personality clashes, or changes and adaptations which we rebel against. The point is that He never gives up on His children.

I have found that the Lord will let me butt my head against the stone wall of challenge until I realize that the wall isn't going to budge. With a bruised and battered spirit, I fall on my knees before Him and ask for a bandage and a ladder. He is the only One who can either break down that wall or boost me over it.

My Grandma, who led me to the Lord when I was very young and knew about my secret childhood dream of becoming a professional writer, told me, "Honey, always write the truth, and don't make God mad!"

The truth I believe God wants me to pass on to you is that every challenge you will face in your marriage is designed not for your hurt, but to strengthen you, your marriage, and, most important, your faith.

"As *for* God, his way *is* perfect: the word of the Lord is tried: he is a buckler to all those who trust in him. For who *is* God save the Lord? or who *is* a rock save our God? *It is* God that girdeth me with strength, and maketh my way perfect" (Ps. 18:30 – 32 KJV).

> Establish a harmonious relationship with your in-laws. This is the eighteenth step in building a marriage that works.

SUGGESTIONS

1. Write your own "in-law" story, touching the high points of your relationship with your mate's family. Has it gone in the direction toward war or peace? Why?

2. Think of something you could do this week to improve the situation, if it has moved toward war. (The

principles in chapters 7 and 8 can help.) If you already have a good relationship, plan to write a note of appreciation to your in-laws, or telephone just to say, "Thanks for being you. I love you!"

PART FOUR

WHAT RESOURCES ARE YOU
DEPENDING ON?

13

IF YOU'D LIKE TO CHANGE

Have we discovered how to change for our own
well-being and for the good of our marriage?

*The Lord my God illumines my darkness. . . . And by my
God I can leap over a wall* (Ps. 18:28, 29 NASB).

We have asked you to consider three key questions
which can make an enormous difference in the quality
of your life:

1. Are your choices moving you in a positive
   direction toward a successful marriage?
2. What kind of emotional climate are you creating together?
3. How well is your partnership working?

In answering these questions honestly, almost
everyone will uncover the need for constructive
change — somewhere, somehow! Letters often arrive

from couples who are at this perilous point. *Perilous* because everything good depends on how they proceed. Will they give up in discouragement? Will they blame each other and demand unilateral change? Or will they take a positive approach, with each partner willing to accept his or her responsibility? And, no less important, will they learn to draw upon spiritual resources for the change that is needed?

If you are at this point, you have plenty of company. When we begin to think seriously about our desires and goals for a happy marriage, we usually find that changes are required both "without and within." Not only do we need to make changes in the ways we relate to one another, but we find that we both need to change on the inside where behavior originates, and that's not a comfortable prospect. It's human nature (the old sin nature, actually) to begin by focusing on the improvements our partner needs to make. The greater our problems, the more loudly we tend to demand change — in the other person. In fact, most people who come for marriage counseling have a hidden agenda which (put in the form of a question) goes something like this: *How can I make my partner change so that I can be happy?* Few of us would voice it so bluntly, but there the belief is, lodged deep within us: If only the other person would change, everything would be all right!

The truth is blunter still. No marriage can work well unless *both* partners are willing to change and keep on changing throughout the long process of establishing their life together.

When your relationship comes right up against this implacable need for change on both sides, it can feel like running into a brick wall. Along with the surprise, hurt, and disappointment come disturbing questions: Will we be able to change enough to make it work? What can I do if my partner won't try to change? And what am I going to do about myself and the ways I need to change? At such times it can look like a wall too high to climb.

If you long to bring about constructive changes in your life, take heart and look at the possibilities. Are you aware of the assets and resources for change which are already available to you — like money in the bank? No matter how you feel at any given moment, the truth is that you are "well-fixed" with assets (valuable possessions and qualities) and resources (sources of aid and support) for transforming yourself, your marriage, and your life. We want to help you learn how to use your assets and how to draw upon the spiritual provisions which can turn the possibilities of your life into shining realities. But please note that these depend upon your eternal connection to the Lord Jesus Christ. If you are not sure of this connection in your life you will need to turn first to chapter 14, to consider the Alpha and Omega choice.

ASSETS AND RESOURCES FOR CHANGE

1. Your Decision-Making Power

We described this asset in chapter 2. You may want to review that chapter after reading this section. Remember that God gave you the gift of freedom of choice by providing you with a will which possesses the power to make decisions based on your best judgment as well as your "want-to" mechanism. And your will was designed to do even more. It has the power to mobilize every part of your being to follow through and carry out your decisions with appropriate actions. Whether you realize it or not, you have the capability of turning your dreams into goals and pursuing those goals to a successful conclusion, even when the way is extremely difficult.

Here is an example of willpower which dramatically illustrates what can be accomplished when we choose to use this valuable asset. The example focuses on mountain climbing, an apt comparison for those of us who have found that straightening out our lives can seem like climbing Mount Everest! In an article entitled "Cold Courage" (*Sports Illustrated,* January 16, 1989), Ed Webster describes the goal he and three other men set: to climb the east face of Mount Everest without Sherpas to carry supplies, and without radios, eliminating the possibility of rescue. They would chart a new and challenging route and make the ascent to 29,000 feet without bottled oxygen. This exercise in courage and willpower kept them moving for days in what climbers call the Death Zone — any elevation above 26,200 feet — where they had to rest after every second step and suffered hallucinations and periods of passing out on the knife-sharp ridges. Their route took them to the South Summit where one man attained the highest peak and Webster obtained incredible photographs; then, eventually, in a prolonged, nightmarish ordeal brought them back down to their base camp past gaping crevasses, their fingers and toes partly frozen, but their lives preserved and their expedition a success.

The steps they took to transform their dreams into attainable goals demonstrate for us what we need to do to achieve the changes we desire: They made their decision; they operated on a belief system, and continually affirmed their beliefs. They prepared themselves through study, training, and practice; they carefully planned their strategy for success; they made sure they had the necessary equipment and supplies; they followed their plan, but adopted new strategies when necessary. They reassessed their goals and acted according to wisdom; they kept their objectives clearly in mind; and they rejected self-pity and kept moving!

Not many of us are looking for adventure of this magnitude. However, bringing about changes in ourselves, our relationship, and the way we live our lives can offer adventure of another sort, equally bracing, sometimes more taxing, and surely more rewarding over the course of a lifetime.

What kind of motivation can impel us to the decision point? What needs and desires can prepare us for this personal "mountaineering" in which all of our being comes together in a positive effort to attain our goals? It often begins with powerful negatives. We are unhappy with ourselves, discontented with our lives, or perhaps, disturbed at what we see happening in our relationship with our marriage partner. We may be painfully aware of our wasted opportunities and discarded dreams, or concerned by our spiritual emptiness, and thirsting for something more.

Just to recognize the negatives will not be enough. Think about it. What do you hear yourself saying at this moment? If you are saying, "I *should* change," you probably won't. The statement implies, "I wish I could, but I can't and I don't choose to try." If you are saying, "I would try to change if only. . .," that's not a good indication either. People who wait for circumstances to change first seldom ever take the positive step. As Thoreau said, "Things don't change. People do." A wishy-washy, indecisive, non-affirmative approach will never pack the power to take you where you want to be.

Instead, begin with a decision. Not the sort of choice one easily, privately, slips into, but a clear-cut, open decision which you will back up with action. The word *decision* literally means "to cut away" so that nothing is ever quite the same again. Once doubts, waverings, worries, and various options which you have considered and discarded are "cut away," your will has the all-clear signal to gear up for action.

Decisions should be stated where others can hear; not kept secret. Sometimes we "think" a decision which seems clear-cut enough, but it can slip away from us when we become distracted by other things. Verbalizing our decision in the hearing of others will help hold us to it, and we need to take advantage of every benefit. It's important to launch our decision with a strong initiative which provides the momentum to establish our choices and turn them into the changes we desire. Thus, action to carry out our decision should be taken or scheduled immediately, for delay can weaken our resolve.

All this adds up to *commitment* — a promise you make to yourself, which others know about. But be careful to state your promise to yourself clearly and affirmatively. When strong negatives motivate you to change, restate them as positive goals. If you're climbing the snowy slopes just to get away from your old self, it will never work. Instead, consider what you are adventuring toward. Merely "to be different" is not enough. What is your goal, your desired destination?

For instance, instead of saying, "I don't want to be fat anymore," set a positive goal: "I choose to find the right balance of eating and exercise to maintain my normal weight — for the rest of my life." Other goals follow, such as these: "I will sign up for the *Eat Slim* class at the local hospital, and go with it all the way until I've reached my desired weight loss," "I will commit one half hour a day to exercise," "I will establish the habit of eating air-popped corn whenever I get a craving for potato chips, or low-fat yogurt in place of ice cream." Note the positive statements. A positive vocalized confession is most important. What you say and what you hear yourself or others say will actually affect the way you think and the way you behave.

Not only be positive about your goal when you speak, but be as precise as possible. Pinpoint it. Only then can you map out a systematic plan to reach a very specific goal. As we have already illustrated, your plan will involve the setting of small goals to be reached one by one as you move toward your main objective.

As you make your plans, remember this: Although feelings will help motivate you to change, do not base your decision or your plans on feelings. That would be like trying to ride on a cumulus cloud. Your feelings can never provide a solid base for progress because they are continually changing — fluctuating day by day and hour by hour. For example, after successfully following a weight-loss program for two weeks, something so upsetting may occur that you *feel* like giving up and going back to your old ways. Fortunately, your will and not your feelings are in charge, so this is the very time to renew the commitment you have made publicly and the private promises you have made to yourself, and to go right on with your adventure.

Ironically, many of us have created our own problems or intensified them by our unremitting efforts to make ourselves *feel* better. The way we humans choose to comfort ourselves can be as unproductive as eating three giant cinnamon rolls because our feelings have been hurt, or arguing with our mate because we've just been chewed out by our boss. We know of even more destructive ways — cigarettes, alcohol, abuse of prescription drugs, and you name it.

Not only do we want to make ourselves feel better. We also want to do whatever we can to avoid taking responsibility for our less than satisfactory situation. That's human nature. Remember how Eve blamed the serpent and Adam blamed Eve, along with God, for giving him the woman? We hate to admit that we alone are responsible for the choices we have made.

But unless we are ready to take full responsibility for our situation, or our reaction to a situation of someone else's making, it will be very difficult for us to achieve constructive changes in ourselves or our marriage. The decision that brings forth a genuine turnaround begins with the recognition that what we have been doing is not working.

When we come to this point, we are ready to search for spiritual resources. And so we look to the next asset which God can give to those who belong to Him, who call Him Lord. That asset is Hope.

2. A Dependable Hope

When believers begin reading the Bible as a personal letter written to them, they find a word scattered like stars throughout the Scriptures, and each time they read the affirmations and promises connected with that word, the sense of encouragement, expectation, and energizing occupies a larger place in their lives. The word is *hope*. It is what we must have to stay on the path of change and make progress.

Here are a few of the verses concerning hope to carry in your mind and heart as life-sustaining equipment. Study them, memorize them, keep them on 3x5 cards in your pocket or purse, or stick them on the refrigerator as a continuing reminder. Mountain climbers say that knowing what to take with them on the climb can mean the difference between success or failure. These Scriptures which keep hope burning in our hearts as a steady flame provide us with one of our most powerful spiritual resources in the quest for change.

> Why are you in despair, O my soul? And why are you disturbed within me? Hope in God, for I shall again praise Him, the help of my countenance, and my God (Ps. 43:5 NASB).

> The hope of the righteous is gladness. . . (Prov. 10:28 NASB).

> "For I know the plans that I have for you," declares the Lord, "plans for welfare and not for calamity to give you a future and a hope" (Jer. 29:11 NASB).

Now may the God of hope fill you with all joy and peace in believing, that you may abound in hope by the power of the Holy Spirit (Rom. 15:13 NASB).

Blessed be the God and Father of our Lord Jesus Christ, who according to His great mercy has caused us to be born again to a living hope through the resurrection of Jesus Christ from the dead (1 Peter 1:3 NASB).

How does hope benefit us? Hope builds and strengthens two valuable aspects of our character which actually determine the way we approach life. The first, *expectation,* makes it possible for us to live with vigorous optimism, and the second, *endurance,* helps us to function with steadfast perseverance. Expectation provides the confidence and enthusiasm to fuel our efforts, and endurance provides the inner steel that keeps us moving forward even when we're tempted to quit. Anyone who has embarked on a program of positive change only to slip back into destructive old patterns of behavior knows that the last state can be worse than the first. Expectancy and persistence founded on biblical hope prevent that kind of devastating backward slide. Expectation keeps us glad, and endurance keeps us going. Both are critical to our success and survival whether we're climbing a mountain or building a love-filled marriage.

Can "hope" really do all that? Yes, if it's biblical hope. The hope God gives us is not an "I hope so." It has nothing to do with wishful thinking. Instead, it means something sure and certain which we anticipate with confidence. Biblical hope has two dimensions. It looks to the future when we can fully enjoy our inheritance in Christ, but it also encircles the present and points to the abundant new life we can enjoy here and now because of Him.

What do you base your hope on? Let's be very practical, for blind hopefulness based on nothing in particular will melt away just when we need it most. Your hope should rest squarely on the fact of the living God and His participation in your life. Every detail of your situation matters to Him. If you are pressed hard by problems right now, if you are longing for changes in yourself, your marriage, and your life, you can count on this: God is in control of everything; God is involved in your problems; God has the answers and provisions you need; and God has promised to provide them for you if you are willing to receive them.

In the beloved classic *Hind's Feet on High Places* by Hannah Hurnard, the heroine collects a bag of small "stones of remembrance," each representing a lesson learned about the Shepherd and His involvement in her life. When she reaches the high places, she discovers that the stones she had gathered — common, ugly stones — have been turned into precious jewels, and the Shepherd reminds her of His promise,

> O thou afflicted, tossed with tempest, *and* not comforted, behold, I will lay thy stones with fair colours, and lay thy foundations with sapphires ... and all thy borders of pleasant stones (Isa. 54:11 – 12 KJV).

If you were keeping a collection of remembrances, what would the contents of your tote bag represent?

There should be at least four kinds of precious stones there, each representing hope for you at this very moment.

First are the promises from God's Word, the Bible. These promises do not fail, for God cannot lie, and there are literally thousands of them in the Scriptures relating to the believer on this earth — plus the heavenly promises relating to the future. Build your hope on God's promises.

The second category consists of the commandments in God's Word. Every command in the Scriptures inspires hope, for God never tells His children to do something that He will not supply the power and direction to achieve. These commandments give added reassurance of His provisions for our daily life. Biblical counselors use this equation:

COMMAND + PROVISION = POTENTIAL FOR CHANGE

In the third category is God's counsel for us through the Scriptures. Because He Himself is our Counselor, we can have hope, knowing that His loving wisdom is committed to guiding and directing us into the paths that will bless us beyond anything we have yet experienced. Sometimes we struggle just to get back to the status quo. But He is able to give us much more than this, and He desires to do it. He wants to be our counselor, to provide us with wisdom for living, and He waits for us to consult Him!

In the fourth category, we find all the ways He participates in our efforts to bring about constructive change. He is the one who actually does the transforming when we cooperate with Him. As we discussed in chapter 2, when God speaks of the changes He will perform in our lives, the Scripture says, "Be transformed," (Rom. 12:2). Note the passive tense of the verb. The work is done in us by none other than the Holy Spirit.

All these reasons for hope are summarized by the apostle Peter who recognizes that God has given us everything we need. Everything.

> His divine power has given us everything we need for life and godliness through our knowledge of him who called us by his own glory and goodness. Through these he has given us his very great and precious promises, so that through them you may participate in the divine nature and escape the corruption in the world caused by evil desires (2 Peter 1:3 – 4).

What about the times when difficulties come at us like driving snow in a blizzard? It does seem that it often happens just when we're trying our hardest and tasting some success. God's Word shows us how the cycle of hope goes right on at such times. The apostle Paul explains,

> Therefore, since we have been justified through faith, we have peace with God through our Lord Jesus Christ, through whom we have gained access by faith into this grace in which we now stand. And we rejoice in the hope of the glory of God. Not only so, but we also rejoice in our sufferings, because we know that suffering produces perseverance; perseverance, character; and character, hope. And hope does not disappoint us,

because God has poured out his love into our
hearts by the Holy Spirit, whom he has given us
(Rom. 5:1 – 5).

The word translated *suffering* in this passage
includes the idea of distresses and pressures. Most of
you know about those kinds of afflictions. The letters
some of you have written to us describe the pressures
and distresses that have invaded your marriage and
your life, but they often lift our hearts with a message of
the peace and victory that we have experienced as a
result of all that has happened. This Bible passage
explains the positive chain reaction that takes place
when we face challenges and difficulties with an attitude of expectation.

First, we expect (*know* by intuition or percep-
tion) that some very good things are going to take
place as a result of the way we meet the difficulty. It's
only by going through the pressures and trials that we
are able to develop steadfastness, the ability to stand
firm under heavy difficulties. This, in turn, develops a
proven character in us that reassures us of our ability
to live with strength and grace in the future, no matter what comes. And that assurance results in even
more hope, a confident hope that God will always see
us through. We don't have to be afraid anymore.
When our hope is centered in God and His promises,
it will never disappoint us (or, as the King James Version says, "put us to shame"). God's love, which
reached out to us when we were unbelievers, helpless
in our sins, continues to pour into our hearts. The
reality of His love in our hearts guarantees that our
hope is not misplaced and will never fail. And so the

cycle begins with expectation and ends with a guarantee.

If you have times of inner distress and feelings of panic, God has a special provision of hope for you. We've been discussing hope as a settled state of mind and heart, and so it is. The Epistle of Hebrews calls it "an anchor for the soul, firm and secure" (Heb. 6:19). But it is also a refuge in times of sudden fear. At such times we need to know that biblical hope is there for us, to protect us and stabilize us. The same passage in Hebrews 6 explains this: "that . . . we who have fled to Him for refuge might have mighty indwelling strength and strong encouragement to grasp and hold fast the hope appointed for us and set before us" (Heb. 6:18 AMPLIFIED).

Undoubtedly, the writer to the Hebrews was familiar with Psalm 25 which reinforces the message for us. The Psalm begins, "To Thee, O Lord, I lift up my soul. O my God, in Thee I trust. Do not let me be ashamed" (vv. 1 – 2). To trust in this way means to be confident; to be sure and expectant; to have biblical hope. In God we place our security: this is a settled state of being.

But even though we *trust*, there still are times when we will fear and flee to God for immediate refuge. The King James Version translates that as *trust*, too. At the conclusion of Psalm 25, we read, "Let me not be ashamed; for I put my trust in thee" (v. 20 KJV). That Hebrew word for trust means "run to for protection": "Do not let me be ashamed, for I take refuge in Thee" (v. 20 NASB). It means that while we live in a settled state of hope, we always have the prerogative of running to God for protection, and this is biblical hope, as well. Whatever your need and condition, God understands and has made provision for it.

Hope is a spiritual resource we cannot do without.

3. The Power of the Written Word

We described the first asset for change (which you already possess) as "decision-making power." Now we want to discuss another kind of power which can operate in your life. This is the remarkable power of the Bible to produce change in people.

Of course, it's neither remarkable nor surprising when we recognize the source of this book. We know from Genesis 1 that God brought the worlds into existence by speaking. His spoken word has power; when He speaks, it is so. We know from John 1 and 1 John 1 that the Lord Jesus Christ Himself is called the Word, who took on human flesh and lived among us; who had only to speak and the waves were calmed or the sick were healed. And from Psalm 119, Hebrews 4:12, 1 Peter 1:23, and many other portions, we know that the Bible is called God's Word, literally, *God-breathed* and written down for us, with the same authority and power to bring order out of personal chaos; peace in the midst of the storms that beset us; meaning to fill our emptiness; and wholeness to heal our hurting, disrupted lives.

The Bible, in short, is a unique book which matter-of-factly claims to have unique power in the lives of those who read it. Even unbelievers respect its wisdom and benefit from it, but only those who come to the Bible with a willing heart can be sure of discovering its dynamic ability to work changes in their lives and transformations deep within their beings.

The Bible works its wonders within us in two phases. First, the Bible has the power to bring us to faith in Jesus Christ; only then can it mold us into new people by working changes in our character, personality, and manner of living which will please Him and bless us. This ongoing change may be dramatic, or as steady and imperceptible as the warming of winter into spring, but whether it occurs quickly or slowly, the effects will be far-reaching.

C. S. Lewis illustrates the surprising extent of the transformation by borrowing a parable from George MacDonald. He suggests that we imagine ourselves to be a living house. When we put our faith in Christ, God comes in to rebuild the house. We know a few repairs are needed, and we expect Him to rebuild us into a decent little cottage. Instead, we discover that He is building a palace. He intends to come and live in it Himself!

Look at 2 Timothy 3:15 – 17 to find how these changes are accomplished. First,

> "the sacred writings . . . are able to give you the wisdom that leads to salvation through faith which is in Christ Jesus" (v. 15 NASB).

Once saved, the adventure of transformation begins. The next verse of 2 Timothy 3 reveals the four ways in which the Bible produces beneficial change in us:

> Every Scripture is God-breathed — given by His inspiration — and profitable for instruction, for reproof and conviction of sin, for correction of error and discipline in obedience, and for training in righteousness [that is, in holy living, in conformity to God's will in thought, purpose and action] (2 Timothy 3:16 AMPLIFIED).

The Scriptures (1) instruct us, (2) reprove us, (3) correct us, and (4) train us. At first glance, these four processes may seem to overlap, but in reality they fulfill four distinct functions, each essential for permanent change.

First, they *teach* us. The Scriptures teach the truth about the way God designed human beings to live and love. As we read the Bible we are instructed by word and example so that we can understand what God's standard is for our life and faith, our character and conduct. New norms are set; we have something to model after, a standard for measuring ourselves, and goals to reach for.

Second, they *reprove and convict* us. The process is not comfortable, but it is beneficial. The word used for "reproof" is a legal term meaning more than to accuse; it includes the meaning of trying a case to its end *successfully*. This is one case we will never win. The Scriptures show us how we have failed to live by God's requirements, and as they hold up a mirror in which we see our own sin, the sight flattens us to the dust. The beneficial result? Repentance! It is only when we recognize how far removed we are from God's design for His creation and how far away we are from the standards set for His redeemed people, that we can begin to change.

Third, the Scriptures *correct* us. They have halted the negative drift of our life. Now they can reset our direction by putting us on our feet and pointing us in the right way. The word for "correction" means literally "to stand up straight again." The Bible has knocked us down; now it lifts us up and gets us moving toward God and all good things. It has wounded us; now it heals us.

It has plowed us up like fallow ground; now it plants us and promises a beautiful harvest. The Holy Spirit, through the Scriptures, not only helps us put off sin like a falling of withered leaves from the tree, but enables us to put on righteousness like a new green growth pushing off the dead remnants of our old life.

The concept of "standing up straight again" speaks to many of us. In a time of self-searching, one woman sadly concluded that she was like a sack that was all fallen together. Another woman responded, "I felt like that too. But the Scriptures are helping me to stand strong and straight!"

Finally, the Scriptures *train us in righteousness*. They literally "child-train" us in a new way of living in which we walk in God's ways until they become our own. If we did not have this final phase of training, we would soon revert to old, destructive habits. But the Holy Spirit, by means of the Scriptures, lovingly disciplines and works with us until our new character reaches maturity.

And what is God's purpose in this four-phase program? It is briefly stated, but all encompassing:

> That the man of God may be adequate, [well-fitted and thoroughly] equipped for every good work (2 Tim. 3:17 NASB).

God wants to make us *adequate* — a wonderful word! It is translated "perfect" in the King James Version, but most of us do not expect perfection: We would be glad to be completely adequate in the living of life. Actually, the Greek word *artios*, which is used only here in the New Testament, means "complete" as an instrument with all its strings, or a machine with all its parts, or a body with all its limbs, joints, muscles, and sinews in good working order. If we give ourselves to the Scriptures, they not only make us complete and thus adequate, but they also equip us for what we will be called to do. The picture is that of a ship being properly fitted out for the voyage. We can be properly equipped for our personal journey through life, if we choose to allow the Scriptures to do their work within us. Remember, the choice is always ours.

4. Your Ability to Form Habits

This is a natural resource everyone can use, but we tend to take it for granted. Think, for a moment, how many of your daily activities are guided by habit. Because God has given us the ability to form habits by repetition, we are able to move smoothly and automatically through most ordinary tasks, with freedom to think about more important matters while we brush our teeth, make the morning coffee, stop at red lights, or, for example, perform our work at the computer on the job.

Originally we learned how to do those tasks and performed them self-consciously until they became an extension of ourselves. It took longer to learn to drive or use the word processor than to fill up the coffee-maker. But we gained these skills by means of consistent practice. If we should move to England, we would have to establish a new habit of driving on the other side of the road. It would not be comfortable at first, but we could soon learn. If we begin using a new program on the computer, it requires careful thought and repetition until we master it. We find the process tiring or challenging at first, but soon it has become second nature and we're back on "auto pilot" again.

This capacity to learn to respond unconsciously, automatically, and comfortably is a tremendous asset when we want to change ourselves or the way we live. Knowing how to "put off and put on," thought patterns and behaviors is really the key to change, according to the New Testament. But the process can be misused, for our habit-forming capability makes it easy to establish harmful patterns of thought and conduct without realizing what we're doing. William James observed that if we realized the extent to which we are mere walking bundles of habits, we would give more attention to what we are forming. Now our challenge is to replace destructive patterns of living with positive, beneficial ones. When we choose to do this in conjunction with the transforming work of the Holy Spirit and the guidance of the Scriptures, our potential for success is great.

Sometimes people have the despairing belief that their personality cannot be changed. Personality is simply the sum total of what we are at any given moment. The Bible views it as a changeable factor which depends, first, upon what we believe, what we affirm, and the way we think. "As [a man] thinketh in his heart, so is he," the Scripture says (Prov. 23:7 KJV). If we habitually fill our minds with faith and biblical principles and set positive goals before ourselves, our behavior will inevitably change to reflect our thinking. As we establish new constructive patterns of behavior, our feelings will invariably correspond. Eventually, (sooner than we might expect) others will notice "a personality change."

Biblical counselor Jay Adams writes of a man who had formed the habit of saying sarcastically, "Oh great!" whenever something failed to go his way. Recognizing that his personality was reflecting a complaining spirit, the man chose to *put off* that behavior and *put on* a positive spirit of praise, no matter how he felt. He began substituting the expression, "O great . . . is Thy faithfulness!" (Lam. 3:23 KJV). After a time of consistent practice his new response became habitual (a part of him), and his attitudes and feelings changed. Now his personality could be described by others as "upbeat" — even radiant.

The question is, how can you take the spiritual resources and natural assets which we have described and use them to produce desired changes within yourself or your marriage?

First, you must diagnose the problem. What do you want to change? (Remember that you are seeking to change yourself, not reform your marriage partner.) What behaviors, responses, and attitudes are not working in your life? What do the Scriptures say about them? Get help on this if necessary.

Second, when you have diagnosed the problem and understood the counsels of Scripture in this area, then target the habitual practice or pattern of response that must be unlearned — *put off*. The only way to do this effectively is to replace the old habit with a new one — *put on*. Decide on the biblical alternative and make that your goal which you will promptly put into action, practicing the positive new behavior until it becomes automatic and habitual. If you need to develop a new attitude, you must find the corresponding action which expresses the new attitude and act it out immediately and consistently. Never let a rosy glow of feeling and high resolve dissipate without acting upon it. You will have lost momentum that will be difficult to regain.

Third, structure your situation for the changes you desire. To know how to do this you will have to give some thought to what seems to trigger your undesirable thoughts and behaviors. You may want to keep a record of the times during the day when they occur. What stimuli do you respond to? If you analyze the behaviors you want to change, you will notice that they develop in a series of steps, or links in a chain. You must break a link in the process to prevent the undesirable behavior. That means developing a new response to the same old situations. The circumstances of your life may not change, but your response to them *can,* and that will make all the difference.

Fourth, to build a new response and break the old chain of habit, you will need to develop your own helpful techniques and search out scriptural affirmations which apply to your situation. All depends on your beliefs, so check them out. Are they rational or irrational? Do they line up with biblical principles? If not, change your beliefs.

One man says he pictures a tool box full of beliefs and affirmations. He says he needs a lot of them to cover the needs of his life — a 1,000-piece set as opposed to a 100-piece set. "Could I repair the Queen Elizabeth II with one rusty screwdriver?" he asks. "Not only do I expand my 'tool box' of truth, but I throw out the rusty, unworkable ideas that I collected along the way — ideas that really make no sense. I want my attitudes and actions to be controlled by beliefs that I know are trustworthy and true."

If, then, you want to change yourself, your relationship with your mate, or any other part of your life, you will need to set systematic goals and have a specific plan to form specific desirable habits which will replace undesirable patterns of thought and behavior. What you *believe* will lie at the heart of any positive change. But while you are taking constructive steps toward change, you may have periods of discouragement and sudden strong temptations to simply quit and slide back into old habits, old ways, old sins. This is the time to draw upon the spiritual resource the Bible calls "help in time of need."

5. Spiritual Help

It's always important to have the assurance that the Lord offers you the resources you need, and it is even more critical at a time when you are taking action to bring your life into line with God's design for you. Do you know the Lord as your great high priest who once lived on this earth as a man and has now gone into Heaven where He is "seated at the right hand of God" (Col. 3:1 NASB) to intercede on your behalf?

Please consider the following scriptural passage very carefully. It can make a great difference in your life.

Therefore, since we have a great high priest who has gone through the heavens, Jesus the Son of God, let us hold firmly to the faith we profess. For we do not have a high priest who is unable to sympathize with our weaknesses, but we have one who has been tempted in every way, just as we are — yet was without sin. Let us then approach the throne of grace with confidence, so that we may receive mercy and find grace to help us in our time of need (Heb. 4:14 – 16).

As you have quietly read these verses today, what do they tell you that can make such a difference? First, *you are not alone.* The Lord speaks on your behalf, acts on your behalf, and represents you before the throne of God.

Not only that. He *understands you.* Because He lived on this earth as One who was not only God but fully man, He knows what this life is like. He is able to sympathize with you, to feel with you in times of weakness and pain, and to feel the reality of the temptations you face. In fact, His capacity for compassion is greater than anyone else's, for He is the only man to have ever fully resisted temptation and to have felt the full extent of its force.

Third, He *has the power to help you.* He is sovereign God who sits on a throne of power.

Fourth, He *has invited you to come to Him.* His throne of power is the *throne of grace,* and He gives you freedom to come to Him confidently to pour out your needs and your heart before Him.

Fifth, because He is God and thus Spirit, *you have access to Him at all times.* You can draw near to Him at any moment in prayer, in thought, in the depths of your inmost being, and know that He hears you.

Sixth, *you can be sure of finding mercy at His throne of grace.* This mercy is the indescribable experience of God's pardon, acceptance, and love.

Finally, *you obtain special grace which is precisely*

suited to your need of the moment. The Greek word literally means "well-timed help." He will strengthen your inner life at the moment of temptation. He will answer your cry for help. When the way of change seems long and hard, He will give you the patience and perseverance to take that next step and the next and so on. When you are hurt because your marriage partner does not recognize the efforts you have made, and it seems your efforts are in vain, then He understands and strengthens you with the kind of strength that no human being can give.

You can count on this special grace and well-timed help to meet you at the point of your need because your faithful and compassionate High Priest makes this commitment:

> God is faithful (to His Word and to His compassionate nature), and He (can be trusted) not to let you be tempted and tried and assayed beyond your ability and strength of resistance and power to endure, but with the temptation He will (always) also provide the way out — the means of escape to a landing place — that you may be capable and strong and powerful patiently to bear up under it (1 Cor. 10:13 AMPLIFIED).

THE WAY OF SPIRITUAL GROWTH

As we try to produce change in ourselves while drawing on spiritual resources, we encounter a principle of life that seems to contradict itself. Nevertheless, it is true, and so we call it a paradox of the Christian life.

The paradox consists of these contradictory facts:

1. To change demands my concentrated effort.
2. God does it for me.

To understand how this can be, think of the psalmist's affirmation, quoted at the beginning of this chapter: *By my God I can leap over a wall* (Ps. 18:28 NASB). To leap over a wall demands tremendous effort on our part: Our feet and our legs and the rest of our body (and mind!) do the work. But God puts the spring in our feet and the lift in our legs. Because of Him, we can clear the barrier, no matter how impossible it may seem when we first consider it.

The Christian life requires all the consistent, concentrated effort we can pour into it, and yet God does it for us and in us and through us. While we "work on ourselves" from the outside, He works on the inside, deep within. We call this spiritual growth, and through this process we are transformed.

The Greeks had a word for this change of condition and character which we still use: *metamorphosis*. This describes the happening when *the outward appearance becomes comparable to the inner reality*. How can the earthbound caterpillar become an exquisite flying creature? The metamorphosis occurs because on the inside he already *is* a butterfly even when he looks like a woolly worm.

What are we on the inside and what are we becoming? If we have trusted Jesus Christ as our Savior and Lord, we already carry a new life within us which is sure to produce new growth in its season. God progressively changes us into His likeness so that our outward expression of character and personality correspond more and more with the inner reality of our life in Christ.

We cooperate in this adventure through the exercise of our choices. C. S. Lewis has said that every time we make a choice, we are turning the central part of ourselves into something a little different from what it was before. Adding up all the choices, we are becoming either a heavenly creature in harmony with God and self and all creation — or a hellish creature that is at war with everything including itself. When we make choices, we are deciding more than the quality of marriage we shall have; we're choosing quality of life for time and eternity.

Spiritual growth means positive change! The New Testament resonates with the possibilities of growth and progressive change into something more glorious. We are assured that

> we all, with unveiled face beholding as in a mirror the glory of the Lord, are being transformed into the same image from glory to glory, just as from the Lord, the Spirit (2 Cor. 3:18 NASB).

If you continue to look at Him with the gaze of faith, you will become like Him. Thus, change in yourself, your relationships with others, and the way you live, will require faith as well as obedience. As the old hymn wisely says, "Trust and obey, for there's no other way. . . ." Real faith in the Lord always expresses itself in obedience to His Word. Your side of the change process involves both obedience in choosing the behavior and attitudes that will produce the best conditions for spiritual growth, and faith that trusts the Lord to accomplish in you what He has promised.

His side of the change process? We hope you will

experience it for yourself in the days and weeks ahead!

Are there desires of your heart which have been awakened or strengthened while you have been reading *Secret Choices*? We want you to know that we are praying with you concerning this. God will fulfill the desires for good which He has placed in your heart.

Our prayers for you are very specific, and we know that these requests are according to His will because we are following the biblical pattern of Paul's prayers for his friends at Philippi.

Paul began by expressing his confidence that the Lord who had begun a good work in them would never give up halfway through, but would continue the positive change process until "the day of Christ Jesus." We are equally confident that the good things the Lord has begun in you will be carried through to a successful completion. We believe He will do even more for you than you ask or think at this moment.

Here is what we are asking for you at the Throne of Grace: first, that God's wonderful agape love will increase in your heart until it fills and overflows your life to bless your marriage partner and many other lives.

Second, we pray that you will grow in the personal knowledge of the Lord Jesus Christ, gaining a clear vision of His beauty and character, and receiving insight into all His ways. We especially ask that you will apply what you read in the Bible and practice it in your own life on a daily basis.

As you translate the Bible into your personal experience, we pray that you will develop discernment, the ability to distinguish between good and evil; between

things that are helpful and things that are not; between
what is of benefit and what is subtly wrong and potentially harmful.

Third, we pray that you will develop the capability
of understanding *what matters* — the literal wording of
Paul's prayer. We ask that you will learn how to choose
well between better and best, in order to make the best
choices in your life; that you will always put your seal
of approval on the very best because it has met the standard of the Word of God. We pray that you will look
beyond what is merely good to find what the Lord's will
is for your life.

We also ask that you will develop the joy of living
which comes from sincerity that is unafraid of the bright
sunlight shining on all its actions. We are requesting
that the Lord will enable you to build pure, unmixed
relationships, and that He will protect you from being a
stumbling block to others, especially your own mate.

And, finally, we pray that as you grow spiritually,
you will be filled with all the fruits of righteousness
which are from Jesus Christ, particularly the fruit of the
Spirit. We ask that the love, joy, peace, patience, gentle-
ness, goodness, faith, humility, and self-control which
characterized our Lord will be seen in your own personality; that you will be strengthened to live out His
love and grace through all the days of your life; and that
you will see His glory.

These are very personal requests, for the process of
change under the Lord's guiding is an intimate one-on-
one experience with Him. Neither of you can do it for
the other one. But we know this: If even one of you puts
yourself in the Lord's hands, He will use that to bless
your marriage.

Commit yourself to the process of change where change is needed, and draw on spiritual resources to bring it about. This is the nineteenth step in forming a marriage that gets better and better.

SUGGESTIONS

1. Decide what changes would most improve your marriage. List three, remembering that change must begin with you alone, unless your partner is equally motivated. What behavior patterns are involved? What do the Scriptures counsel in these circumstances? (Use *Secret Choices* along with our other books, *Intended for Pleasure, Love Life,* and *The First Years of Forever* as reference sources.)

2. Make your own list of "put-offs" and "put-ons" from the Bible, beginning with the New Testament epistles. In your notebook, fill in three columns headed

Put Off   **Put On**   **Scriptural References**

Use your habit-forming ability to make these changes a part of you. Remember that even desirable changes make us feel uncomfortable at first, like a fish out of water, until we have formed the new habit and expanded our self-image to correspond with our new behavior.

3. Write out your own plan for personal change, following the general pattern set by the Mount Everest climbers. Make each phase a matter of prayer, keeping a record of requests, answers, temporary setbacks, and victories.

4. Mark Philippians 1:9 – 11 in your own Bible and read it daily for a month. This is our prayer for you. Assess your life one month from today and thank God for what He has already done, and thank God for the progress you already see.

> And this is my prayer: that your love may abound more and more in knowledge and depth of insight, so that you may be able to discern what is best and may be pure and blameless until the day of Christ, filled with the fruit of righteousness that comes through Jesus Christ — to the glory and praise of God (Phil. 1:9 – 11 AMPLIFIED).

14

THE ALPHA AND
OMEGA CHOICE

> Have we met the eternal One, the all powerful
> One? Have we heard His invitation? Are we able
> to draw on the resources of the living God for
> every need of our life?

*I am Alpha and Omega, the beginning and the ending,
saith the Lord, which is, and which was, and which is to
come, the Almighty. . . . And whosoever will, let him take
the water of life freely* (Rev. 1:8; 22:17 KJV).

We have been discussing personal choices that can
take you in the direction you want to go — choices
which will make it possible for you to build a marriage that lasts and that wholly satisfies both of you
for a lifetime.

In the first chapter we described the three dimensions of a successful, satisfying marriage, and in later
chapters we outlined the choices involved in creating
an emotional climate of love, nurturing, and intimacy,
and in forming a smoothly working, enjoyable partnership. The third dimension is a faith you can share — a

vital faith in God's Son, Jesus Christ — and your choice in this area is the most important one you will ever make.

More than any other choice in life, it is a solitary one. It involves your willingness to make connections, first, with the living God, and then with your marriage partner on the deepest level possible, but only you can arrive at this decision, and you must come to it alone. Others can give you helpful information, but you must decide, in the privacy of your own heart, what to do with the truth when you read it or hear it spoken. Doing nothing is also a choice with eternal consequences.

It's possible that many of you have already acted on the truth and responded to God's gracious invitation through His Son Jesus Christ. If so, you know the benefits of your shared faith, and the fulfillment you find together in His love. We know, from personal experience and from the testimonies of hundreds of married couples, that it is this shared faith which gives marriage its meaning, stability, and settled joy over "the long haul" of a lifetime. It also provides the spiritual resources we need in the course of our years on this earth and assurance for our future.

We would like to give you information that can assist you in making a choice, if you have not already done so. Others provided this information for us, and we are passing it on. In Dr. Wheat's busy world as a family physician, a concerned patient told him about the Lord Jesus Christ, and his life dramatically changed course. In Gloria's case, her family directed her to the Bible where, as a young wife, she met Jesus Christ along with the woman who came to touch the hem of His garment. And so she made the choice which has shaped her life and work.

Come with us to the last book of the Bible which opens with these words: *The revelation of Jesus Christ.* He is the subject of this book which presents Him as He truly is: the King of Kings and Lord of Lords.

A revelation means an unveiling or a disclosure. Let's consider the disclosures made here concerning Jesus Christ, a man whom the world respects, but does not understand.

1. He is the eternal One who is the beginning and ending of all things.

> I am Alpha and Omega, the beginning and the ending, saith the Lord, which is, and which was, and which is to come, the Almighty (Rev. 1:8 KJV).

The man whom the world considers a good, humble man and a wise teacher is much more: He is God Himself, the eternal, self-existent One. Alpha and Omega are the first and last letters of the Greek alphabet, indicating the fact that Christ is before all creation and will continue to exist after the present creation is destroyed. Other Scriptures tell us that all things were created by Him and for Him. (Read Rev. 21:5 – 6 and 22:13.)

> For by him were all things created, that are in heaven, and that are in earth, visible and invisible, whether they be thrones, or dominions, or

principalities, or powers: all things were created
by him, and for him: And he is before all things,
and by him all things consist [hold together]
(Col. 1:16 – 17 KJV).

In the beginning was the Word, and the Word was
with God, and the Word was God. The same was
in the beginning with God. All things were made
by him; and without him was not any thing made
that was made. In him was life; and the life was the
light of men (John 1:1 – 4 KJV).

2. He is the Almighty, the all-powerful One.

I am Alpha and Omega,. . . the Almighty
(Rev. 1:8 KJV).

The man whom the world saw meekly dying a
criminal's death on a Roman cross — and forgiving
those who participated in His death — is none other
than the "Lord God Almighty," the *pantokrator* who
controls all things and possesses all power and authority in heaven and earth. (Read Rev. 4:8; 11:17; 15:3;
16:7, 14; and 2 Cor. 6:18.)

His name is called The Word of God. . . . He tread-
eth the winepress of the fierceness and wrath of
Almighty God. And he hath on his vesture and on
his thigh a name written, KING OF KINGS, AND
LORD OF LORDS (Rev. 19:13, 15, 16 KJV).

That at the name of Jesus every knee should bow,
of things in heaven, and things in earth, and
things under the earth; and that every tongue

should confess that Jesus Christ is Lord, to the glory of God the Father (Phil. 2:10 – 11 KJV).

3. He is both the eternal One and the resurrected One.
Fear not; I am the first and the last: I am he that liveth, and was dead; and, behold, I am alive forevermore, Amen; and have the keys of hell and of death (Rev. 1:17 – 18 KJV).

After dying on the cross and spending three days in a tomb guarded by Roman soldiers, Jesus demonstrated to all people for all time that He is God by rising from the dead — one of the most legally authenticated facts of history. He spent more than a month on this earth in His resurrection body, seen by hundreds of people including the disciples who became vibrant witnesses of the Resurrection, willing to give their lives for the truth. He then ascended to heaven as many witnesses watched, with all power and authority in His possession, including authority over death and the place of the dead. The Christian's death and resurrection are both in His hands.

For I delivered to you as of first importance what I also received, that Christ died for our sins according to the Scriptures, and that He was buried, and that He was raised on the third day according to the Scriptures, and that He appeared to Cephas, then to the twelve. After that He appeared to more than five hundred brethren at one time, most of whom remain until now, but some have fallen asleep; then He appeared to James, then to all the apostles; and last of all, as it were to one untimely born, He appeared to me also (1 Cor. 15:3 – 8 NASB).

But we see Jesus, who was made a little lower than the angels for the suffering of death, crowned with glory and honour; that he by the grace of God should taste death for every man. . . . Forasmuch then as the children are partakers of flesh and blood, he also himself likewise took part of the same; that through death he might destroy him that had the power of death, that is, the devil; and deliver them who through fear of death were all their lifetime subject to bondage (Heb. 2:9, 14 – 15 KJV).

4. He loves us! The eternal and almighty God loves us.

To Him who loves us . . . (Rev. 1:5).

For this reason, Jesus Christ came to earth to live as man and to taste death for us so that we might have everlasting life. If we believe this, and enter into an eternal relationship with Him, nothing can separate us from the love of Jesus Christ.

For God so loved the world, that he gave his only begotten Son, that whosoever believeth in him should not perish, but have everlasting life. For God sent not his Son into the world to condemn the world; but that the world through him might be saved. He that believeth on him is not condemned: but he that believeth not is condemned already, because he hath not believed in the name of the only begotten Son of God (John 3:16 – 18 KJV).

Who shall separate us from the love of Christ? . . .
In all these things we are more than conquerors
through him that loved us. For I am persuaded
[completely convinced], that neither death, nor
life, nor angels, nor principalities, nor powers, nor
things present, nor things to come, nor height,
nor depth, nor any other creature, shall be able to
separate us from the love of God, which is in
Christ Jesus our Lord (Rom. 8:35, 37 – 39 KJV).

*5. When He died for us on the cross, He set us free from
our sins by shedding His own blood.*

To Him who loves us and has freed us from our
sins by his blood . . . (Rev. 1:5).

At a specific moment in history, Jesus Christ, the
only man who ever lived without sin, chose to die by
crucifixion in order to bear the sins of the whole world
and pay the death penalty for them. Through that
mighty act, planned in eternity past, He opened the way
for all our sins to be forgiven. In Jesus our sins are forgotten as though they were put in the depths of the
deepest ocean and remembered no more. And we need
never be under the dominion of sin and at its mercy
again. He is called the Savior for He has saved us from
our sins. On our side, it is required that we believe on
Him and what He has done, and receive Him as our
Savior and our Lord.

The Father . . . hath delivered us from the power
of darkness, and hath translated us into the kingdom of his dear Son: In whom we have redemp-

tion through his blood, even the forgiveness of sins (Col. 1:13 – 14 KJV).

But as many as received him, to them gave he power to become the sons of God, even to them that believe on his name (John 1:12 KJV).

6. He has given those who believe on Him a new identity and a new purpose which is life-transforming.

From Jesus Christ the faithful and trustworthy Witness, the First-born of the dead (that is, first to be brought back to life) and the Prince (Ruler) of the kings of the earth. To Him Who ever loves us and has once (for all) loosed and freed us from our sins by His own blood, And formed us into a kingdom (a royal race), priests to His God and Father, to Him be the glory and the power and the majesty and the dominion throughout the ages and forever and ever. Amen, so be it (Rev. 1:5 – 6 AMPLIFIED).

We are a special people — special because God has chosen and preserved us for Himself. His purpose. That we will live in His wonderful light as witnesses to His glory and grace.

But you are a chosen race, a royal priesthood, a dedicated nation, (God's) own purchased, special people, that you may set forth the wonderful deeds and display the virtues and perfections of Him Who called you out of darkness into His marvelous light (1 Peter 2:9 AMPLIFIED).

7. *He makes all things new for the believer.*

> And he that sat upon the throne said, Behold, I
> make all things new. And he said unto me,
> Write: for these words are true and faithful
> (Rev. 21:5 KJV).

Salvation and new life come through believing in
Jesus Christ, the Son of God, as our Savior and receiving
Him by faith. When we put our trust in Jesus Christ and
our lives link up with His, we become new people. Our
problems may seem the same, but our ability to cope
with them is all new. We have a source of love beyond
ourselves. We have a sufficiency of grace for every situation. We have a new kind of strength from the power of
the Lord Jesus Christ that manifests itself through our
own weakness. We now have the ability to behave in the
ways that will bring an abundance of blessing and order
into our lives. We discover new wells of creativity and a
new zest for adventure with God.

> Therefore if any man be in Christ, he is a new
> creature: old things are passed away; behold,
> all things are become new. And all things are of
> God, who hath reconciled us to himself by
> Jesus Christ (2 Cor. 5:17 – 18 KJV).

8. *He offers the water of eternal life to anyone who is thirsty.*

> It is done. I am Alpha and Omega, the begin-
> ning and the end. I will give unto him that is
> athirst of the fountain of the water of life freely
> (Rev. 21:6 KJV).

We have called this the Alpha and Omega choice, because the eternal and all-powerful God who is at the beginning and ending of our life, and who encompasses all that is in between, gives us a gracious invitation: "If you are thirsty, come and drink freely of the waters of eternal life. Come to Me and drink and be satisfied."

If you are thirsty, come and drink.

Is it really that simple? A Bible teacher once said, "The questions that matter in life are remarkably few, and they are all resolved by coming to Him."

But how do we come? How do we receive Him by faith? The Scripture explains,

> The word is near you; it is in your mouth and in your heart, that is, the word of faith we are proclaiming: That if you confess with your mouth, "Jesus is Lord," and believe in your heart that God raised him from the dead, you will be saved. For it is with your heart that you believe and are justified, and it is with your mouth that you confess and are saved. As the Scripture says, "Anyone who trusts in him will never be put to shame." For there is no difference between Jew and Gentile — the same Lord is Lord of all and richly blesses all who call on him, for, "Everyone who calls on the name of the Lord will be saved" (Rom. 10:8 – 13).

Where does our faith come from? Scripture explains,

> Faith comes from hearing the message, and the message is heard through the word of Christ (Rom. 10:17).

And so we have given you the message straight from the Scriptures. The Word of Christ is clear and plain. God, who is "the root and fountain of all being" loves us with a personal, everlasting love that has made provision for us to belong to Him. This is possible because of the sacrifice of Jesus Christ which paid the penalty for our sins, past, present, and future. The Lord Jesus Christ is not only the eternal One and the all-powerful One: **He is the all-sufficient One who waits to meet every need of our life for now and through all eternity.**

We find that because He is the eternal One, life has continuity; life makes sense. We find purpose and meaning and vitality in living. It is not just that we have entered into Life; Life has entered into us. God is doing something in us and through us, and it will go on forever.

We find that because He is the almighty One, He is in control. Our life is never again out of control. He is at the helm, and works all things for our eternal good. He holds us together even when we feel as though we are falling apart, for He is our center point.

We find that because He makes all things new, we have a wonderful sense of freshness and newness and hope. We find that His mercies never come to an end: They are new every morning.

We find that because He is our all-sufficient Savior, we are never alone. We are delivered even from the burden of ourselves. He Himself is our environment, and we can trust Him for everything we will ever need on earth or in heaven.

Here is a prayer you may want to follow in expressing your faith in Jesus Christ as your Savior:

> Heavenly Father, I realize I am a sinner and cannot do one thing to save myself. Right now I believe Jesus Christ died on the cross, shedding His blood as full payment for my sins — past, present, and future — and by rising from the dead He demonstrated that He is God. As best I know how, I am believing in Him, putting all my trust in Jesus Christ as my personal Savior, as my only hope for salvation and eternal life. Right now I am receiving Christ into my life. I thank you for saving me as You promised, and I ask that You will give me increasing faith and wisdom and joy as I study and believe Your Word. For I ask this in Jesus' name. Amen.

If you have made your choice and acted upon it, a wonderful new life is before you with the Lord. You will want to seek out other believers and find your own place of worship and service in a local church which clearly teaches the Bible. We hope you will write and tell us, so that we can pray for you by name. We welcome you into the family of God!

The last chapter of the Book of Revelation contains one final invitation. This time the Holy Spirit joins with "the bride" which is the church in extending the invitation to all who will hear. Those who hear are encouraged to respond and to pass the invitation on to others. Will you hear the Lord Christ and receive His gift of eternal life by faith in Him? The choice is yours.

> And the Spirit and the bride say, Come. And let him that heareth say, Come. And let him that is athirst come. And whosoever will, let him take the water of life freely (Rev. 22:17 KJV).

Share your growing life of faith in the Lord Jesus Christ. This is the twentieth—and most important—step in building a love-filled marriage and a wonderful life.

HOW TO USE THE POWER OF YOUR SECRET CHOICES: TWENTY STEPS TOWARD A WONDERFUL MARRIAGE

1. Become aware of your secret choices and discover their power in your life.

2. Establish the picture of the marriage you desire, fill in the details, and keep it fresh in your mind to guide your choices.

3. Remember that *every choice has its consequences* and learn to "count the cost" before you act or react.

4. Understand this basic principle: *your willingness to behave responsibly needs to be coupled with God's power.*

5. Keep your mind renewed and filled with the Word of God so that you can learn how to respond in every situation of marriage according to His good counsel.

6. Study the Creator's original design for marriage, and live by His design.

7. See yourself and your partner as you really are, and love, accept, and delight in your partner on the basis of reality.

8. Make a once-for-all decision to take the path to intimacy and test all you do and say by the question, "Will this draw us closer or move us apart?"

9. Create an emotional climate of caring by finding out what nurtures your partner and then doing it, gladly and lovingly.

10. Put the B-E-S-T plan for nurturing your partner into effect and follow it consistently.

11. Recognize that God is the true source of faithfulness for your marriage, and choose to demonstrate His faithful *hesed* love to your partner.

12. Decide to pour your life into learning the art of loving your mate, and avoid any hint of indifference.

13. Commit yourselves to resolving conflicts in ways that will bring you closer and forge a stronger partnership.

14. Turn the control of your life and the power struggles of your marriage over to God to settle the war once and for all.

15. Share your vision and work out a Master Plan for your partnership.

16. Develop strategies to achieve your goals and carry out your Master Plan.

17. Learn how to manage your money to accom-

plish your goals and to avoid the unhappy consequences of overspending.

18. Establish a harmonious relationship with your in-laws.

19. Commit yourself to the process of change where change is needed, and draw on spiritual resources to bring it about.

20. Share your growing life of faith in the Lord Jesus Christ.

RECOMMENDED CASSETTES

These may be obtained from your local Christian bookstore or ordered from Bible Believer's Cassettes Inc., 130 Spring St., Springdale, AR 72764. BBC, Inc. is the world's largest *free loan* library of Bible study cassettes with more than ten thousand different teaching cassettes for loan. More than one thousand of these are on marriage and the family. Write for further information.

Wheat, Ed. M.D. *Before the Wedding Night*. An exciting counseling series for the couple planning to be married. One of the world's recognized authorities on premarriage counseling provides the medical, emotional, and spiritual counsel every prospective bride and bridegroom need to hear. These cassettes are also widely used by counselors in working with troubled marriages. Three hours on two cassettes.

Wheat, Ed. M.D. *Love Life for Every Married Couple*. Listening together to this two-cassette album will improve your understanding and verbal communication concerning your love relationship. Three hours of positive counsel to enhance your marriage.

Wheat, Ed. M.D. *Sex Techniques & Sex Problems in Marriage*. In the privacy of their homes, couples are benefiting from this helpful, frank but reverent discussion of sex technique and solutions to sexual problems. Combines timeless biblical principles with the latest medical findings and treatment of sexual dysfunctions. Unanimously acclaimed by Christian leaders. Three hours on cassette.

RECOMMENDED
VIDEOCASSETTES

These are available from Scriptural Counsel, 130 Spring St., Springdale, AR 72764.

Wheat, Ed. M.D. Fooshee, George, and Sanchez, George. *Foundations for a Successful Marriage.* This permanent videocassette resource addresses potential problem areas of sexual maladjustment, family finances, and emotional and spiritual communication. Three counseling sessions, each about 43 minutes.

Wheat, Ed. M.D., and Wheat, Gaye. *The Love Life Marriage Seminar.* The Wheats' popular Love Life Seminar, professionally videotaped before an audience at Coral Ridge Church, Ft. Lauderdale, FL. Includes a television interview with Dr. D. James Kennedy. Six and one-half hours on eight videocassettes.

Ed Wheat, M.D. and **Gloria Okes Perkins** have collaborated on a number of books including *Intended for Pleasure, Love Life for Every Married Couple,* and *How to Save Your Marriage Alone,* as well as the videocassette series *Before the Wedding Night,* forerunner of *The First Years of Forever.* He is a retired physician and sex therapist in Springdale, Arkansas. She is a writer and biblical counselor.